Contents

Acknowledgements

p. 9, p. 13 and p. 20: extracts from the Jerusalem
Bible, published and copyright 1966, 1967 and 1968
by Darton, Longman and Todd Ltd and Doubleday
& Co. Inc, and used by permission of the publishers;
p. 47: extracts from the English translation of *Rite of
Holy Week* © 1970, ICEL, pp. 48 and 50: extracts
from the English translation of *The Roman Missal*
© 1973, ICEL; all rights reserved; p. 49: extract
from the English translation of Creed by the
International Consultation on English Texts (ICET);
pp. 69 and 70: extracts from the English translation
of *Rite of Baptism for Children* ©1969, ICEL; pp. 73
and 74: extracts from the English translation of *Rite
of Marriage* © 1969, ICEL; all rights reserved.
cover photo: Andes Press Agency
photo credits: p. 2: The Image Bank, Sally and
Richard Greenhill, Andes Press Agency, The
Hutchison Library, Format Photographers; p. 3:
Format Photographers, Sally and Richard Greenhill;
p. 4; Rex Features; p. 7: (top two) Andes Press
Agency, (bottom two) Rex Features; p. 10: The
Hutchison Library, Andes Press Agency, p. 11:
Douglas Dickins; p. 12: The Hutchison Library;
p. 13: Andes Press Agency; p. 14: Rex Features;
p. 16: (top two) Hutchison Library, (bottom) David
Richardson; p. 21: Andes Press Agency, p. 23: Andes
Press Agency; p. 24: Format Photographers, Andes
Press Agency; p. 27: Andes Press Agency; p. 30:
(left) The Hutchison Library, David Richardson,
(right) Format Photographers; p. 33; (first six) Rex
Features, Andes Press Agency; p. 34: Sally and
Richard Greenhill; p. 35: Professional Photographic
Services, Andes Press Agency, Format
Photographers, Rex Features; p. 36: Rex Features;
p. 38 (top): Peter Sanders, (bottom) Rex Features;
p. 39: (top) David Richardson, (middle) Jaysons,
(bottom) Peter Sanders; p. 40: Rex Features; p. 43:
Andes Press Agency; p. 45: Andes Press Agency;
p. 46: Andes Press Agency, Mary Evans Picture
Library, Andes Press Agency; p. 47: (left) Topham
Picture Library, p. 48: Andes Press Agency; p. 54:
Sally and Richard Greenhill; p. 59: Frank Spooner
Pictures; p. 65: David Richardson, p. 67: David
Richardson; p. 68: (top) Rex Features, (bottom)
David Richardson; p. 69: Andes Press Agency; p. 71:
Sally and Richard Greenhill; p. 72: (top two) Andes
Press Agency, (bottom) Hutchison Library; p. 73:
Andes Press Agency; p. 74: Andes Press Agency.

3·50

Weaving the Web

Communication Celebration-Values

Level 3

A modular programme of Religious Education

Richard Lohan and Mary McClure SND

Collins

Collins Liturgical Publications
8 Grafton Street, London W1X 3LA

Collins Liturgical in Canada
Novalis, Box 9700, Terminal
375 Rideau St, Ottawa, Ontario K1G 4B4

Collins Dove
PO Box 316, Blackburn, Victoria 3130

Collins Liturgical New Zealand
PO Box 1, Auckland

First published 1989
© 1989 Richard Lohan and Mary McClure

Programme Components

Community, Story, People

Level One	0 00 599149 8
Level Two	0 00 599150 1
Level Three	0 00 599151 X

Communication, Celebration, Values

Level One	0 00 599152 8
Level Two	0 00 599153 6
Level Three	0 00 599154 4

Teacher's Book 0 00 599156 0

The National Project of Catechesis and Religious Education
Published with the authority of the Department for Christian Doctrine and Formation of the Bishop's Conference of England and Wales

Typographical design and typesetting by VAP Publishing Services, Kidlington, Oxon.
Illustrations by Clyde Pearson
Printed by Bell and Bain Ltd, Glasgow

Weaving the Web is a religious education programme which weaves together various strands in the context of the family and the local community, as well as in the wider world, the global context.

A module is about half a term's work, six-to-eight weeks. There are tasks to complete, individual and group work, and there is also the opportunity to assess your own work. Self-assessment lets you know how you are doing as you work through this programme.

For religious people, prayer and worship are ways of keeping in touch with God and ways in which worshippers remember and experience God's concern for them.

If you are new to this programme, WELCOME

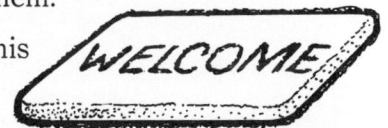

The four strands in
WEAVING THE WEB

Family community
The basic community that people belong to

Local community
The people and places around where you live

Plural community
The variety of people and groups with different beliefs and customs

Global community
People and places worldwide

1

This module of work in your R.E. programme is called

Communication *Level Three*

This module is all about the ways in which people communicate their experiences of the mystery of life.

You will reflect upon your own experience of communication, and you will explore some of the reasons or arguments used to speak about the existence of God.

Here is an overview of the work you will cover in this module. You will:

● **reflect** on the mystery and the importance of life.

● **reflect** on some of the arguments used for the existence of God.

● **explore** the images of God used in Jewish and Christian Scriptures (the Bible).

● **consider** the ways in which Allah is described in the Qur'ān.

● **reflect** on special times as "communication".

● **consider** prayer in Islam.

● **reflect** on the use of symbols as ways of communicating mystery.

● **examine** the Eucharist as an action which communicates thanksgiving and peace-making.

● **assess** and **evaluate** your work.

If you have completed Communication Level Two, here are some of the tasks you did:

- You explored different ways of keeping in touch.
- You analysed the effectiveness of different types of communication.
- You looked at ways in which worship is a way of communicating what people believe about life.

In a sentence, write a definition of communication.

Name three different ways or types of communication.

Now, let's move on . . .

The meaning of life

Most people believe that life is important. Many people find life or the events of life, or the things that happen to them, a mystery at times.

If you have completed the module on Celebrations in Level Two you have already thought about many events like war, illness and death as well as the joyful experiences which are part of life and which are celebrated. There are events or happenings in a person's life which sometimes make it difficult to understand what life is all about.

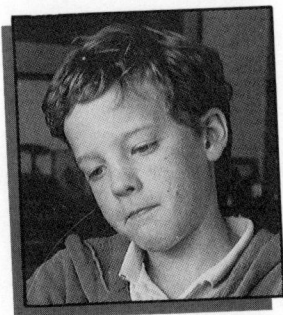

Another way of expressing this is to talk and think about the *meaning* of life.

People talk about the "meaning" of life: let's explore what that means.

The meaning of life is whatever gives life its value and purpose.

Task 1

Make a list of all the things which you care about; which have a value for you.

Make a list of all the people you care about in your family grouping.

Extend your list to include the wider family/the local community/the global or the world-wide concerns which you may have.

Now, reflect! What is life for? What is the purpose of life?

(Perhaps you will want to leave this question until later in the module.)

Extension work

A GROUP TASK
Collate (put together) all the items which you have in your lists. *Display* your findings.

B
What "things" does your school value?
From your experience, who are the people who are valued?
Which global concerns are also your school's concerns?
What is the purpose of school?
How does your class's lists of values compare with the school's values?

The meaning of life

Read the two accounts that follow and then answer the questions.

Jim's Story

" If I had to write about the 'meaning' of life then I would be a bit stuck! What I can write about is the way I spend my time and my pocket-money . . . then you'll begin to know some of the things which are important in my life.

I like my parents and I enjoy the times when we can do things together. My father works on an oil-rig in the North Sea. The money is very good, and he was lucky to get a job after he had been made redundant from the electrical firm where he worked. I enjoy the security that comes from having a father in work. My trainers and tracksuit have famous brand-names on them. We have two holidays a year – one in the autumn half-term and the other in August.

It will now seem a bit strange when I say that being together as a family, spending time together at home, hearing all the things which have happened to my little brother and sisters, even when they go on and on a bit . . . these are the important things: more important than my 'Speedo' leather football and my designer trousers and my . . . well, perhaps, you know what I mean . . . do you?

And when my dad writes to me . . . when I see the Aberdeen postmark on the envelope, I can't wait to open it. Sometimes at night when I lie in bed thinking, I worry about him, especially in the winter months when the sea is wild and the weather is awful . . . "

What are the really important things for Jim?
What kind of relationship does he have with his father, and with the rest of the family?
How important is it for him to be "trendy" or in fashion?
If you were Jim, would you be able to discuss your concerns with an adult?
If you had to write an account like Jim's for "Weaving the Web", what would you write about the "meaning of life" for you?

The meaning of life is what is valued by individuals and groups and what is believed to be the purpose of life.

" I know Jim, the young lad you have been reading about. He's a good lad, for a 14-year-old, he has a wise head on young shoulders, as the saying goes.

I was 14 a long time ago, 50 years ago actually. You may think that 64 is really old, perhaps I'm older than your gran or grandad ... but I still feel quite young! Young on the inside ... when I look in the mirror I see someone who is beginning to get on a bit ... middle age is always about ten years older than I am!

I have a family, four daughters and a son. I have six grandchildren and I love each of them. They are all quite different from each other – John is tall and quiet and is in the third year of his university course. He visits me regularly and never says a word! Jan, his sister, has never been interested in schoolwork. She belongs to a dance group and is keen on all sorts of sport. She visits me as well (never with John) and she always has lots to say. Gary, who is only six, is absolutely spoiled by his older brother and sister ... and by me! Hugh is 17 and is very interested in art and graphic design – he visits when he's a bit short of money ... but it's always good to see him. He often says that all famous artists are, or were, usually short of money! His sister, Sarah, spends her time listening to her personal stereo. She usually visits me when her mum brings her. And then there's Elizabeth (junior!) She's always in trouble at school because she has lots to say ... on almost every subject. Elizabeth loves talking and discussions ... she isn't too keen on settling down to homework ... but she calls in to see me each day after school, 'How are you, gran? Can I make you a cuppa? What kind of day have you had?'

Three years ago, my husband died. It was very sudden, and it was a great shock to everyone. I miss him a great deal, and sometimes I almost forget that he has died ... when our grandchildren visit and tell me their news, sometimes I'm about to say ... 'wait till grandpa hears this ... he will be pleased ...' and then I remember that he has died. And yet, as a Christian, I believe that death is not the end, that somehow, in a mysterious way his love for me and my family continues. His life has been changed, not taken away. My Christian faith gives me comfort and gives me meaning in my life. "

How important is Elizabeth's family for her? Can you identify with any of the grandchildren? Which one and why? What do you think about Elizabeth's belief about "death is not the end"? If death is part of life-experience, what does it mean?

Extension work

A

Already you have had many experiences in your life which are more meaningful than other experiences. Another way of saying this is that some of the things which have happened to you mean more than others.

Write about two happenings or events in your life which mean a lot to you.

Say why these events means so much.

B

Write a short story with the title, "If I had my life to live over again ..."

For many people, the mystery or the meaning of life becomes clearer when there is belief in God. Believers meet or encounter the mysterious God in prayer: "Call to me and I will answer you; I will tell you great mysteries of which you know nothing" (Jeremiah 33:3). Just like the prophet Jeremiah, believers today experience that through prayer they can become aware of God's presence, and God can communicate with them.

Task 3

Imagine that you had a ten-minute interview with God.

Write down five questions which you might ask God.

Now compare your questions with the rest of your group. If you have any questions which you prefer to keep private then do not share them.

Were there any similarities in the types of questions which emerged?

What were the differences?

Extension work

A

Choose two of the issues or concerns which were mentioned.

Are there any answers? If so, what are they?

B

How would you respond if someone said that "prayer is keeping in touch with God"? If you had to explain this to a 9-year-old, how would you explain it in a letter?

Task 4

Read the poems or word-pictures below. They describe two of the seasons of the year. Give each poem a title and then write, or draw or make music or dramatise the other two seasons.

"Sun and freckles and lots of sneezes.
Smells and sounds of cut grass and more sneezes and watering eyes.
Dark glasses and cans of coke
– the real thing –
over-heated bodies squeezed into last year's, now too small blazer. **"**
Eileen Year 3.

"... cancelled football and crunching sounds beneath my fur-lined boots, cold toes and nose; white breaths and pounding heart as I run for the bus which is already late.
Bright lights, cold nights, warm house ... longing for holidays ... **"**
Jason Year 3.

Extension work

A

Which season of the year do you enjoy most? Give reasons for your answer.

Which season of the year do you enjoy least? Give reasons for your answer.

B

If a person's life could be summed up as four seasons from birth to death what would be the spring of a person's life, the summer of a person's life, the autumn of a person's life and the winter of a person's life?

To make sense of the world, many people believe that there is a Source or Designer of the world, which they call God.

Read the following:

Many people look at the world which is ever changing and yet there is an order or pattern to the way things are. In Task 4 you reflected on the order or pattern of the year – spring, summer, autumn and winter. You also thought about a person's existence from the beginning of life to its end, in terms of four seasons. (Extension work B.)

Each day has its own pattern: day and night/light and dark/ morning and evening.

Many people ask, "Where does the pattern or the order that is in creation come from? Where does the design come from?"

A scientist may answer that the order or pattern comes from the law of physics.

Another person might ask, "But where does the law of physics come from?"

And so, the questions about the meaning of life and existence go on . . .

Extension work

A

A reflective task! Where can you see order or pattern in creation? *Find out* about the life-cycle of a plant or insect. *Display* your finding to the rest of the class.

B

The pattern or order which can be seen in creation and in life is sometimes used as a "proof" that God exists. The above argument is called the "Argument from Design". Because there is order and pattern in creation there must be One who orders or patterns creation. This Source or Designer is called God.

What do you think about this argument?

Is it a convincing argument for the existence of God? Give reasons for your answer.

More about the Argument from Design

This "argument" which for some people is a way of proving or pointing to the existence of God, also helps people to come to terms with or explain something of the mystery of life.

Just as there is a pattern or order in the created world, so too there can be a pattern or order in an individual's life.

For a person who has belief in God, the events in her or his life, as well as in the world at large, are not meaningless.

In prayer, which is one of the ways in which a person communicates with God and God communicates with the individual, there is an opportunity to try and understand the meaning of this pattern in their lives.

Read the following excerpt from a newspaper article.

MAIREAD'S RETURN

Mairead Boyle, volunteer nurse with "Voluntary Service Overseas" (V.S.O.) contacted her parents yesterday for the first time in 22 weeks. They thought she was dead. They heard that the mission station where she worked had been attacked by guerillas and that all foreigners had been taken off into the bush. Now they know exactly what happened to her.

Mr. Boyle told us in an exclusive interview, "Mairead was taken hostage and, with four others, was marched through the jungle. They walked over 200 miles in the blistering heat. When she rang, after having been freed, she said that there was not a time in the whole experience when she felt that she would die. 'When you are walking, in silence as well as in the dreadful heat, and there is no shelter and lots of time to think, you have plenty of time to reflect on your life. We were not badly treated, although there was no doubt that we were their prisoners.' "

When asked what kept her in good spirits and gave her the courage to go on, Mr. Boyle replied: "This is what we asked her. Mairhead replied, 'I felt that God was very close to me . . . that somehow, here in the middle of the jungle, I was being cared for, looked after. You may think it's strange, but in spite of the heat and the ordinary fear that comes from not being free to do what I wanted, there were times when the actual beauty of the jungle was overwhelming: the colours of plants, the exotic birds . . . I knew that if God cared for creation in this way, everything would work out.' "

Answer the following:

Mairead's story

Knowledge
What was Mairead's profession?
Which agency did she work for?

What are volunteers with "Voluntary Service Overseas"?

How long was Mairead "out of touch" with her family?

What conclusion had her family reached about her?

Understanding
Why do people join organisations like "V.S.O."?

Why was Mairead unafraid?

In this newspaper article there is an example of someone's conviction about the existence of God.

What strengthened Mairead's conviction about God's presence in her life?

Evaluation
What do you think about Mairead's experience?

Imagine how you might have felt if this had happened to you.

Write down some of your imaginings.

What did Mairead's family make of their daughter's experience?

Extension work

A
How does the Argument from Design appear in Mairead's experience?

B
Do some research! *Find out* about a Voluntary Agency which sends people abroad into what might be dangerous situations. *Write* to the Agency and see if there is a possibility of inviting a speaker to your class who will talk about her/his experience.

or

Read the "seven ages of man" from Shakespeare's *As you like it.* (Ask your teacher of English to help you find the speech!) What is the life-pattern suggested by the seven ages of man? *Dramatise* the seven ages.

ASSESS your work!

Remember, assessing your work is an important part of the R.E. programme. It is an opportunity for you to see how you are doing, and also to have some feedback from your teacher.

Tasks 1–6

If you had to explain to someone what "the meaning of life" meant, how would you do it?

In these tasks you have read some people's personal stories. Which story did you like? Why?

How would you explain what the Argument from Design was all about?

Did you do any of the extension work?

Ideas about God

Task 7

Read the following:

Many people believe in God and believe that God communicates with the believers. Worship is an expression of this conviction or belief in God.

Reflection

This task is a quiet reflective one. Read the excerpts below. Each one is taken from the Bible which contains the sacred books of two major world religions. (Which ones?) Christians regard the Bible as the Word of God expressed in human language – not dictated by God word for word, but inspired by God in order to express the message of God's concern for all of humanity.

Words, of course, are not enough by themselves to make communication possible. Words have to be listened to. (Prayer can be a form of listening). Words often demand a response. The different quotes here convey various ideas about God. Study them carefully, then decide with a partner what each is trying to convey.

"God created man in the image of himself, in the image of God he created him, male and female he created them." (Genesis 1:27)

"Yahweh is great and supremely to be praised in the city of our God." (Psalm 48:1)

"I shall not call you servants any more, because a servant does not know his master's business; I call you friends, because I have made known to you everything I have learnt from my Father." (John 15:15)

"Courage, my daughter, your faith has restored you to health." (Matthew 9:22)

"How great is your name, O Lord our God, through all the earth! Your majesty is praised above the heavens . . ." (Psalm 8:1)

"In the wilderness too, you saw him: how Yahweh carried you, as a man carries his child, all along the road you travelled on the way to this place." (Deuteronomy 1:31–32)

Extension work

A

If you were asked to draw a picture of the image presented for each, what would you draw?

B

Do any of these images of God appeal to you?

Which ones and why?

God is with us

Task 8

In the previous task, you began to explore and reflect upon some of the images which are used to portray what God is like. The images or pictures of God were taken from the Old Testament. Some words of Jesus were also given.

For Christians, Jesus Christ is the image or the likeness of God. Another way of saying this is, that in Jesus, in his way of living, in his way of dying which showed his love for humankind, and in his way of being present wherever "two or three are gathered together in his name" . . . in all of these, Christians can come to know God. Jesus is called "Emmanuel", which means "God is with us". In Jesus, Christians encounter and meet God.

Look at the image or icon used alongside. Saint Paul said "He is the image of the unseen God."

Extension work

A

Do some research! *Find out how icons are made, and also who paints them.*

Then make a selection of icons which you find interesting.

B

Find Luke 15:3–7. The parable of the lost sheep. What image of God is presented here? Retell this story, using the same image of God, but make the story modern . . . as if it were happening today, in your school or your area.

If you have time, act out your modern parable.

More about Jesus as the image of God

Task 9

Has anyone ever told you that "you're the image of your mother/father/auntie . . . whoever?"

Write down all the people that you are supposed to resemble or be like.

Now, was the likeness physical? Do you have your grandfather's curly hair? Your aunt's double chin? Your mother's blue eyes? Whatever?

or

Do you have the same even temper as your aunt? Your grandfather's quick temper? Your mother's sense of humour? Whatever?

Being like someone can refer to physical likeness or to personality likenesses.

In the previous task when you considered how Jesus was the likeness of God, it did not mean that Jesus looked or looks like God.

What it means is that in the words and actions of Jesus, in the concerns that Jesus showed in his everyday life, and in the concerns which the Christian Church has today . . . in all of these Christians come to know what God is like, and what being a true disciple demands.

Just as words communicate a message when they are listened to, so Jesus communicates God. St John says of Jesus: "The Word was made flesh, he lived among us, and we saw his glory" (John 1:14). St Paul describes Jesus as "God's Yes . . . the Yes to all God's promises" (2 Corinthians 1:20). Christians believe that in Jesus God speaks to them.

Jesus is God's word.

Extension work

A

You will need plenty of time for this task.

Start with the Gospel of Luke. Skim through the chapters of this Gospel and then *note down* the kind of people that Jesus was concerned about/or spent time with. The concerns of Jesus are the concerns of God.

B

Christians believe that in the person of Jesus they are in contact with God.

Invite a Christian from your area to speak to your class about her/his faith in God?

The Names of God

Task 10

Find out about the 99 beautiful names of God in Islam: the Plural dimension of this programme.

Look at the poster.

In a mosque, a place of worship for Muslims, there are no statues or pictures or images of Allah, God, or of Muhammad, the Prophet of Allah.

It is against the Holy Book of Islam, the Qur'ān to try to make pictures of Allah. But Muslims do have ideas about what Allah is like and how Allah would like them to live.

Ninety-Nine Names of ALLAH

The Beautiful Names

AṢ-ṢAMAD
The Eternal

AL-HĀDĪ
The Guide

AL-ḤAKAM
The Judge

Extension work

A

Write to or *arrange* a visit to a local mosque and find out what words are used to describe Allah.

B

Here are three of the "beautiful names of Allah".

What do they tell you about Allah?

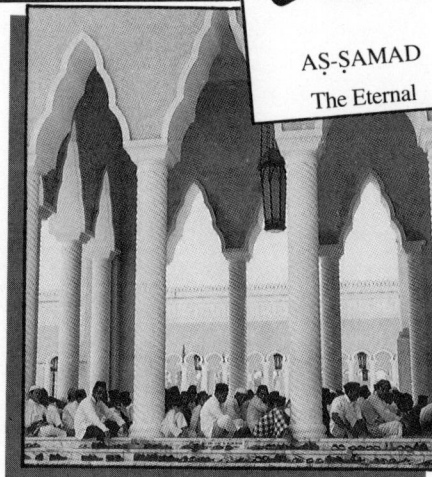

Remember: For Muslims, the Holy Qur'ān contains the actual words of Allah which were recited to the Prophet Muhammad by the Angel Gabriel.

Tasks 7 – 10

1. *What is an icon?*
2. *How are icons used?*
3. *In which ways is Jesus the "image" of God?*
4. *Recall three of the "beautiful names of Allah".*

5. *Recall one Old Testament image used to describe God.*

Did you do any extension work?

Before you move on to the next tasks, have you any work or tasks to complete?

Exploring communication

Task 11

Read about Jack and Alice

Answer the following:
1. *Name the different stages which Jack's and Alice's relationship has passed through.*
2. *How do you get to know others?*
3. *Give an account of a relationship with someone that you have got to know over a period of time.*
4. *How do you feel if you have to listen all or most of the time?*
5. *How much silence do you experience in class?*
6. *Do you value silence?*

Extension work

A

Interview a couple and ask them to reflect on the first time they met, and how their relationship developed.

B

"There is a time for speech and a time for silence."

What does this mean?

When can silence be good or productive?

JACK AND ALICE

Jack often thought about the first time he met his wife. It was a Saturday evening. He had not really wanted to go to the disco, but went along anyway. On his way home that evening he met Alice at the bus stop. She was waiting for the 50 bus. It was late, and the buses were few and far between. He let his own bus go because he wanted to talk to Alice. There were about half a dozen people waiting, and there was a friendly atmosphere. Alice didn't often go to discos . . . she found the music too loud and the lights gave her a headache. Jack admitted his own dislike of the noise and lighting.

As Alice was boarding the bus, Jack asked if he could see her again. She called out her telephone number as the bus trundled off. All the way home, Jack kept saying the number over and over again in case he forgot it. Jack phoned Alice on the following Sunday afternoon and they arranged to meet. They discovered that they had many interests in common. They took a long time to get to know each other. They talked and listened to each other a lot, and sometimes they just sat in silence with each other.

Even now, married for ten years, there are times when they sit together with nothing to say, except be in each other's company. Jack once read a poster at the back of church which said, "If you do not understand my silence, you will not understand my words". At first, this confused him; now he knows what the poster means.

Special times

Task 12

Let's explore "special times".

The poem alongside is taken from the Book of Ecclesiastes, Chapter 3:1–11.

By yourself, or with a partner, think and write about, a "time when you laughed and a time when you cried"; "a time for seeking and a time for finding"; "a time when you felt uprooted".

Think of a time in your life when it was right for you to keep silent, and another time when it was right for you to speak.

Can you think of any "special times" which are not mentioned above?

> " For everything there is a time
> a time for everything under the sun.
> A time to be born and a time to die;
> a time to plant and a time to uproot;
> a time to tear down and a time to build up;
> A time to weep and a time to laugh;
> A time to seek and a time to find;
> A time to be silent and a time to speak . . . "

Extension work

A

Write about a "special time" in your life.

B

Compose your own poem along the lines of the quotation from Ecclesiastes.

A time for prayer...

Task 13

A young person I know gets up early every morning to pray before he sets out for his training school placement. He says: "If I didn't plan to have that time first thing in the morning I would probably just have a lie-in until the last possible moment. I want to have time for prayer . . ."

Julie is in fourth form and spends some time each day in prayer: "I started to pray about two years ago . . . before that I thought I was praying but I was just 'saying' my prayers. Now, I sit quietly and try to mean what I say. Sometimes I read a passage from Scripture to get me going."

I know a teacher who spends 15 minutes of his lunchbreak in the school chapel. "I need time to be quiet and to reflect. Some days I teach and see over 200 faces . . ."

Abram gets up very early each morning to perform "salat" – the ritual prayer in Islam "I suppose it just seems natural to me, like breathing – I just do it. It is an important part of my faith as a Muslim . . ."

A religious Sister is part of a praying community: "At seven o'clock every morning we meet together to pray. We say the Morning Prayer of the Church which contains three psalms, a reading from Scripture and prayers for all those in need. Then there is breakfast and then the members of my community go off to their various jobs: nursing/social work/teaching and parish visiting.

When we return in the evening, we meet together again and say Evening Prayer. It is important for us to pray together and to remember that we hope to be working for God during the day."

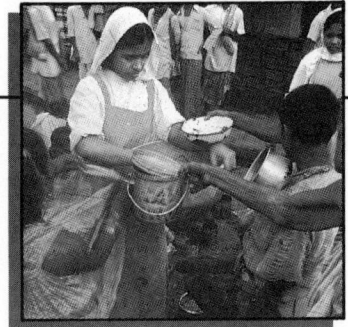

What do you think about these examples of people who pray?

Do you know of anyone who makes time to pray regularly?

What about you?

Why has each person above "made time" for prayer?

Extension work

A
Case Study
Find out more about people who pray by contacting a Religious Order whose main "work" is to pray, for example Camelites/Poor Clares/ Carthusians . . .

B
Can a person pray when working/cycling/listening to music/washing dishes?

What are your views on this?

Why would these times be popular times for those who decide to pray: early morning/lunchtime/before and after work/before going to bed?

A time for worship

Task 14

In worship, those who take part believe that keeping in touch with God is very important. In fact, keeping in touch is essential.

As people who want to get to know each other spend time together, so too, worship is a way of getting to know God or keeping in touch with God.

Find out at which times and on which days of the week there is worship in two places of worship, for example, a Christian church or a mosque.

What is the significance, if any, of the set days and set times for worship.

Worshippers believe that God communicates through the events of everyday life with its ups-and-downs, as well as in and through creation, the natural world; through the sacred Scriptures and also through formal as well as informal prayers.

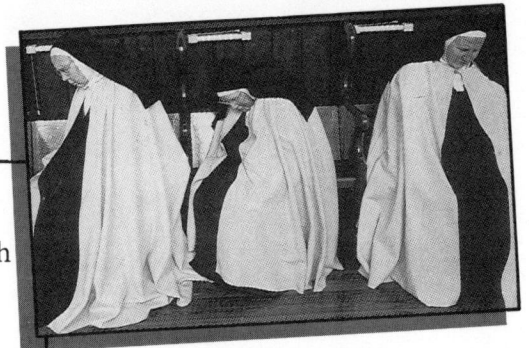

Extension work

A
If you were a worshipper, what would be a good time for you, and why?

B
Reflect on the ups-and-downs of life.

At what times of life might it be easier to believe in God, and at what times might it be difficult to believe in God?

Tasks 11–14

In these tasks you explored communication further and you also reflected on special times in your life and in worship.

1. *What makes one time "more special" than another?*
2. *Write about a "special" time in your experience which may not have been "special" for the other people who were present at the time.*

Did you do any of the extension work?

What did you enjoy most in these tasks?

Can you think of any way you would improve this part of the module?

Before you move on to the next Tasks, look over your work and complete any work which is incomplete.

A look at Islamic worship

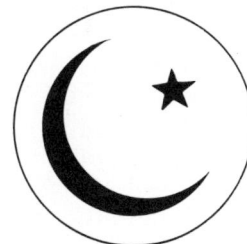

The word Islam means "submission". Islam is about submission to God, Allah, and God's divine will – everything which God wants.

Islam was founded by the prophet Muhammad, and the purpose of Islam is to be at peace with God by acting obediently, by listening to God in every part of one's life.

The word Islam also means peace. Islam means peace and it brings peace.

Task 15 Reflection

Think of the different meanings of peace, for example, peace in the world; peace at home; peace with oneself.

Now, reflect more deeply about "peace with oneself". This may be a bit difficult.

Have you ever felt restless?

What caused your restlessness?

What did you do about your restlessness?

What brought you peace?

Extension work

A

What is "peace of mind"?

Write a short story around this theme.

B

For the religious believer, peace comes when the person is "right with God". Being "right with God" comes from acting and living in a way where God is the priority, the most important or first concern of the person. There are many examples of people who lived restless lives until they found peace with God.

Do some research! Here are some starter ideas for you. *Find out* about the life of St. Augustine before he was a saint; St. Paul; Muhammad . . . or a holy man or woman.

Summary

In Islam, God comes first in everything. Every action a Muslim performs is called Ibadah. All of life can be religious.

Religion is not confined to special places or times: these are important but the whole of life is important, work, play, law and worship.

The Five Pillars of Islam

In a previous module you may have read about the Five Pillars of Islam.

If you have, what can you remember about them?

Read the description below and check your memory.

If you are not sure about the Five Pillars, then read what follows.

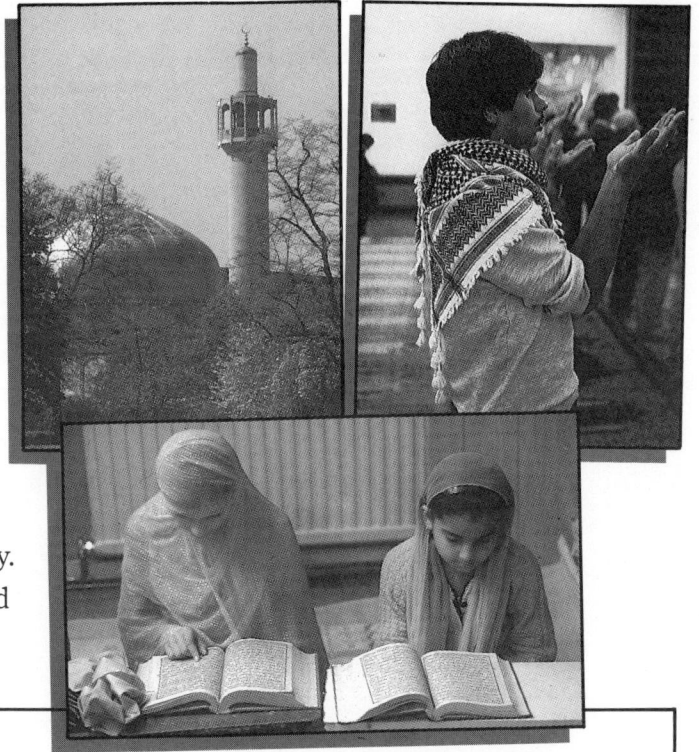

Task 16

Read the following:

Islam has five basic duties which Muslims must perform. These are called the "Five Pillars", and are mentioned in the Hadith which contains the sayings of the Prophet Muhammad.

The first is Shahadah – the declaration of faith that there is only one God, Allah, and that Muhammad is the prophet of God.

The second is Salat – the five compulsory daily prayers. In task 18 you will look at Salat more closely.

The third is Zakat – this means that a Muslim contributes 2½ per cent of personal wealth to those less fortunate, every year.

The fourth is Saum – this is the fasting from food and drink during sunlight hours during the holy month of Ramadam.

The fifth is Hajj – every Muslim should try and make a pilgrimage to the holy places associated with the life and ministry or work of the Prophet Muhammad.

Now answer the following questions:

How many basic duties are there for a Muslim?

Why are they called the "pillars" of the Muslim faith?

What would you think about contributing 2½ per cent of your pocket money every year to those less fortunate than you?

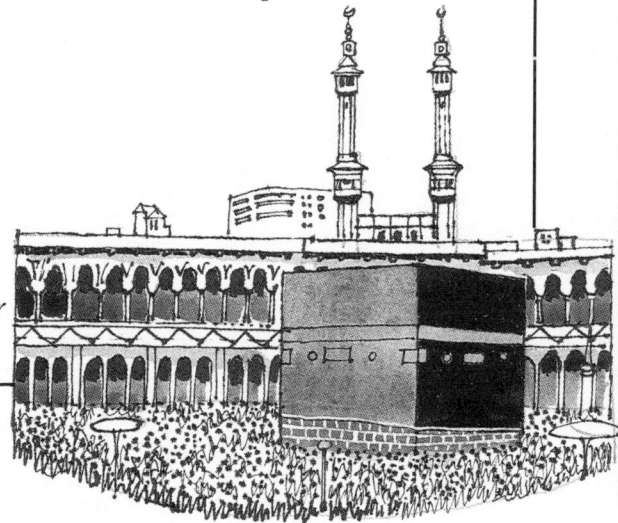

Extension work

A

Write to the Islamic Education Centre in London for further information about Zakat or *do some research* in your school library.

B

Find out about the activities which take place during Hajj and why these activities are an important part of pilgrimage.

Preparation for Salat

Task **17**

Read the following, and then using your own words explain what happens during Wudu.

WUDU

Before beginning prayer, a Muslim must prepare him/herself. Women usually pray at home. This preparation is called *WUDU* or *WUZU*. (Wudu or Wuzu means *to wash for prayer.*)

This preparation involves ritual washing. Wudu is an exercise which helps the person concentrate on the importance of prayer. Before prayer, the Muslim purifies him/herself from any defilement, that is anything which would make the person unworthy to come into contact with Allah in this special way.

First, hands are washed, then mouth and nose before the whole of the face.

Then the right hand and forearm as far as the elbow, then the left. Then the head is wiped with the hands and finally the ears and feet.

It says in the Qur'ān:

"Believers, when you rise to pray, wash your faces and your hands as far as your elbows, and wipe your feet as far as the ankle" (Surah 5:6).

Extension work

A

Why do Muslims prepare for Salat in this way?

What does it say about the importance of Prayer?

B

What occasions would prompt you to wash yourself, apart from everyday washing?

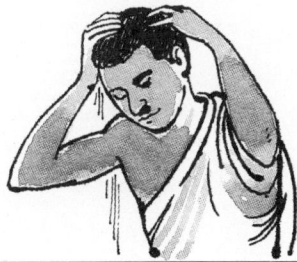

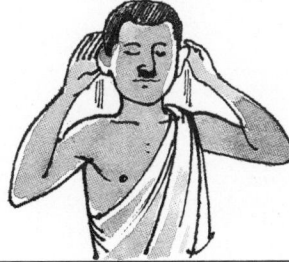

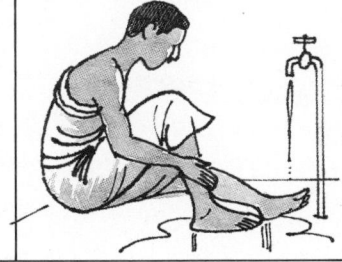

Salat – regular worship

Task 18

For Muslims, prayer is not just the repetition of set prayers which have to be said five times a day, it also involves certain movements or prayer sequences.

In Muslim countries, a man called a MUEZZIN calls the people to prayer with these words:

> **"** The *Adhan* [call to prayer].
> God is great. [*said four times.*]
> I bear witness that there is no God but Allah. [*twice.*]
> I bear witness that Muhammad is the Messenger of God. [*twice.*]
> Come to prayer. [*twice.*]
> Come to security. [*twice.*]
> God is most great. [*twice.*]
> There is no god but God. [*twice*]. **"**

The *Adhan* is whispered in the ear of a young baby. The pray-er faces Mecca. If the person is not in a mosque, the prayer mat is unrolled and placed on the ground. The prayer sequence RAKAT is performed five times each day. It is illustrated here.

1. Allahu Akbar [God is the greatest].
2. Recite Qur'ān. Allahu Akbar.
3. Glory be to my Lord the Great.
4. Allah listens to whoever thanks him.
   Our Lord thanks be to thee.
5. Glory be to my Lord the most High.
6. I bear witness there is no God but Allah.
7. 8. } The Muslim recognises that there are others at prayer.

Extension work

A
Draw the prayer sequence.
Make a list of the Arabic words and their meanings. Why pray REGULARLY?

B
Why **bow** in the presence of Allah? Why **kneel**? Why touch the ground with one's **forehead**? What do these gestures **mean**?

ASSESS your work! — Tasks 15–18

1. *What are the five Pillars of the Muslim faith?*
2. *Write a sentence explaining what each Pillar is about.*
3. *Why is Salat important?*
4. *What preparations must take place before Salat is performed?*
5. *What times are prescribed for Salat?*

Did you do any extension work?

Revelation as communication

Christianity starts from a revelation. The word "revelation" is connected with the word "reveal". Christians believe that God has revealed himself to human beings.

For Christians, this revelation of God is in the person of Jesus Christ.

Christian worship revolves around Jesus, the messenger, who is also the message, a message of salvation.

Answer the following questions:
1. *What does "revelation" mean?*
2. *In what sense do Christians believe that Jesus is the revelation of God?*
3. *What do you think is meant by "the messenger is also the message"?*

Being "saved" or being freed from certain situations is an ordinary human experience.

For Christians, salvation is from sinfulness. Sin separates people from God. Sinfulness is often selfishness and greed of individuals and communities. Personal sin is turning away from Jesus' way of living. Communities and societies can be selfish and greedy and so cause wars, violence and injustice.

Christians believe that Jesus frees them from sin in order to love and serve others. The Christian message is one of liberation – being freed from sinfulness and selfishness in order to be freed to act like Jesus and create a world of justice and peace. This entails a struggle since liberation is never easy. In the sacrament of reconciliation Christians reflect on the way they live, accept God's love and forgiveness and promise to take up the struggle with greater dedication, having re-centred their lives on God's love. Reconciliation is a gift of God, who wants people to be free and at peace.

Do you think that for those who wish to live as Jesus did it will entail a struggle? In what ways?

Extension work

A

Explore what "saving" means.

Have you ever been saved from anything? Drowning? Falling? . . . What? *Write* about the experience.

How do you understand the Christian belief that Jesus liberates human beings?

B

Compose a brief speech or sermon addressed to Christians on the theme of "Jesus the Liberator". Outline what you consider people and communities might be freed from in order to be free to follow the way of Jesus.

Compare your thoughts with those of others in the class.

Christians believe in a God who communicates

Task 20

Read the following excerpt from the Letter to the Hebrews which is part of the New Testament.

> 66 At various times in the past and in various ways, God spoke to our ancestors through the prophets. But in our time, in the last days he has spoken to us through his Son. He is the radiant light of God's glory and the perfect copy of his nature. 99 (Hebrews 1:1–4).

In the above the author of Hebrews has a clear understanding of what God is like: God communicates or "speaks" with people. God communicates. This passage also speaks of Jesus Christ as the "communication" of God; this is what God is like – God is in the person of Jesus Christ.

There were many communications in the past, but now Jesus is God's word or communication.

Extension work

A

Find John's Gospel Chapter 1 verse 14.

Write out the whole of the verse and then say how it relates to what the author of the Letter to the Hebrews has said.

B

Recall two incidents from the life of Jesus.

What do they say about God?

Write why you chose those two and not any others.

Sacred time

Task 21

For Christians, time is used symbolically – what is called the Christian calendar or the liturgical seasons.

Look at the calendar alongside and reflect on the way the different liturgical seasons represent the important events in the life, death and resurrection of Jesus Christ.

What is remembered about Jesus at Advent/ Christmas/Lent/Easter/Pentecost?

Find out what "Trinity Sunday" celebrates.

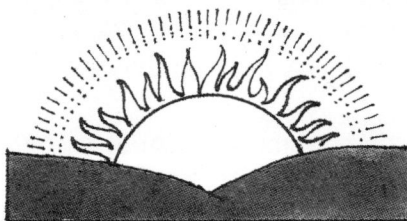

Places of worship are symbolic meeting-places for encounters with the God who is worshipped there.

Look at the design of several Christian churches. Why do they have: steeples? Arch-shaped windows? An altar-table? Candles? A circular or cross-shaped building? The architecture of places of worship communicates what things are remembered and important in worship.

Make a display of your findings.

Ritual actions are symbolic of the attitudes which the believers have in the presence of God.

Perhaps you will remember reflecting on symbolic actions in Communication Level Two.

What do the actions below symbolise in the context of worship?

Extension work

A and B

Display some of the work you have done in a local church or in your classroom.

ASSESS your work!

Tasks 19–21

1. *What is Revelation?*
2. *What is a liturgical calendar? What does it commemorate?*
3. *How is the use of gesture a means of communication in worship?*
4. *Did you attempt the role-play? How did it go?*
5. *"For Christians, God is a God who communicates". What do you understand by this?*

Did you do any extension work?

Look over the last few tasks, is there any work which needs completion?

When you have completed your work, move on to the next tasks.

How did we do?

Communication is a way of being present to others

How can you keep in contact with people who are not with you at the moment? You thought about this in Communication Level One.

As human beings with thoughts and feelings as well as bodies, we need to communicate what we think and feel to others. This is a way of keeping in touch or of being present to others.

Read the following story of Ian's recent trip to London:

"I never knew that so many people could be crushed into one compartment of the underground train. I felt like a sardine. It was five p.m. – rush hour. There was hardly breathing space. The strange thing was that no one said a word. I was a bit embarrassed, I was so close to complete strangers. The thing was – there was absolutely no communication. I was glad to get back home!"

Were the travellers present to each other?

Were they in communication with one another?

"I remember the year I spent the whole summer with my grandmother. She lives on one of the remotest islands off the west coast of Scotland. I stayed the whole summer because I had managed to break both wrists when I flew off my bike – head first! Of course, I put my hands out to save me . . . wouldn't you? Anyway, I was glad to get away from home. My school friend saw me off at the airport. She made me laugh, 'Keep in touch,' she called.

How could I, unable to write and no telephone at my gran's?

One day, a piece of my plaster cast sort of broke off. (I was trying to get on a bike at the time!) I asked my gran to put it in an envelope and send it to Karen.

Gran did. I received a letter within the next week . . ."

What do both stories say about "being present" to others?

Extension work

A and B

Write a short story which illustrates that communication is about being present to others.

The Roman Catholic Eucharist or Mass

Roman Catholics believe that, in four ways, God is present in the community which gathers for worship:

- In the people who come together as a community.
- In the Word of God.
- In the priest who leads the worship.
- In the sacrament of the body and blood of the risen Lord Jesus.

In a special way, God communicates in four ways: People/Word/Priest/Sacrament.

Task 23

Draw a symbol for each of these ways of communication.

Extension work

A

If worship and prayer are ways of communicating with God and also ways in which God communicates, then decide which of the following statements are true for Christians.

1. God is remote.
2. God is interested in human beings.
3. God is very close.
4. God communicates in a variety of ways.
5. God has no sense of humour.

B

The statements below are about Christians. Do you agree with them?

1. Christians should not get too involved in life.
2. Christians should enjoy themselves.
3. Christian worship is an escape from reality.
4. Christians have a lot to be thankful for.
5. Christians should communicate good news.

The Roman Catholic Eucharist or Mass explored through
symbol, sign and gesture

The word "Mass" came from the last words said by the priest. Until about 20 years ago, the language of the Mass was always Latin. This language was intended to be a common language for worship. It ensured that wherever there were Catholics, there would be uniformity in the way the Mass was celebrated.

The last words of the Latin Mass were, *"ite missa est"*. From these words, the Mass got its name.

Eucharist is a Greek word which means thanksgiving. The Mass is about thanksgiving. You will explore this later in the module.

Communities need to come together because it is a way of keeping in touch with each other and with God.

Faith communities, groups of people who share the same beliefs need to come together to give each other support, to worship together, to remind one another that they "belong" to each other and to the global community.

Gathering and celebrating.

In pairs answer the following questions:
Why do people come together?
Name some occasions which prompt a family "get-together" or reunion.
Why does the Catholic community gather together?

Catholics come together for a purpose:
- To maintain links with God and one another.
- To listen to God's word.
- To be strengthened to go out into the world and bring the good news to others.

Gathering together

At the Eucharist, the people, young and old, families and those who are not married, gather together in one place, usually a building which has been set aside specifically for that purpose – a church.

The people sit together. The priest welcomes the congregation with open arms. Open arms are a symbolic gesture of welcome.

As a community which tries to live the way Jesus taught, there is time at the beginning of the celebration to reflect on what has happened during the week.

The priest leads the people in an act of sorrow.

Many people show their sorrow by bowing their heads or "beating their breasts" as a symbol of sorrow for the times they have failed to live and act in Christian ways ... for the times when they have not loved enough.

"For the times when we have been selfish: Lord have mercy."

"For the times when we have been slow to forgive others: Christ have mercy."

"For the times when we have not listened to your word: Lord have mercy."

As a sign of God who is always ready to forgive, the priest raises his hands in blessing over the people:

"May the Lord have mercy on us, forgive us our sins and bring us to everlasting life. Amen."

These symbolic gestures prepare the people and the priest to listen to God's word in the readings from the Old and New Testaments.

God "speaks" through the words of Scripture.

Task 25

In your own words, describe what happens at the beginning of the Eucharist.

Do the symbolic gestures "work"? Do they convey what they are supposed to mean?

Extension work

A

Interview two people who attend the Eucharist. Ask them about the beginning of the celebration and what it means for them.

B

How would you make this part of the service meaningful if there was a celebration of the Eucharist in school?

The Eucharist as thanksgiving for creation and salvation

Task 26

Think of five things that you are thankful for.

Here are some ideas to start you off: good health freedom to think as you like a home . . .

In the Eucharist thanks is given to God for creation.

At every Eucharist, the worshipping community gives thanks to God for the whole of creation.

Some members of the community take up the "offertory gifts" of bread and wine.

Bread is a symbol of human life: it represents human work. As bread is made by human hands and as many grains of wheat were ground together to make a loaf, so too the Christian community is made up of many people throughout the world.

Wine is a symbol of joy and celebration. The wine has also been made by human hands and is the result of many grapes being crushed together.

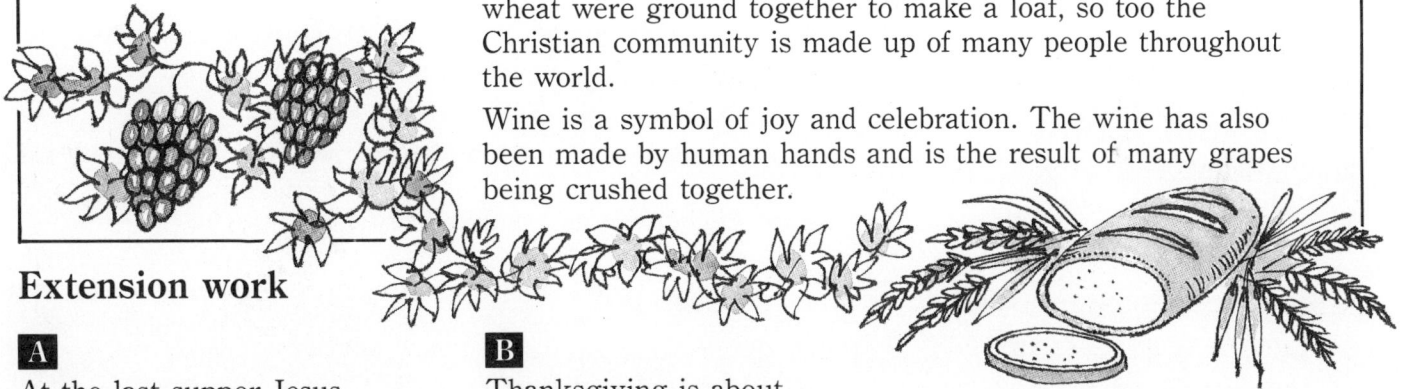

Extension work

A

At the last supper Jesus celebrated with his disciples on the night before he died, bread and wine played an important part – as we shall see later. Jesus told his friends, "Do this as a memorial of me" (1 Corinthians 11:25).

Why are bread and wine appropriate symbols for Christians to use to represent the joys and achievements of human life?

B

Thanksgiving is about returning thanks for what has been received.

For Christians, creation is a gift from God. God's creative power or spirit is present in creation. Human beings have a duty to care for the earth. *Compose* a poem or hymn of thanksgiving on our duty to care for the earth.

RECALL

Meals are special ways of remembering special events. In Judaism, the most important event in Israel's history is remembered when the Passover is celebrated.

The Eucharist as sacrifice

Task 27

When celebrating the Eucharist, Catholics recall and re-enact the story of Jesus.

In St. John's gospel, chapter 13, it says that, "while they were at supper he got down from the table, tied a towel around his waist and began to wash his disciples' feet".

They were surprised to see Jesus act like a servant, and Jesus said that they too had to become like servants of other people.

Read this account for yourself.

At the passover meal Jesus took bread and blessed it and said, "Take this and eat this all of you, this is my body given for you". Then he took the wine and said, "Take this and drink it all of you, this is my blood which will be given for you. Do this in memory of me".

Jesus offered his life for his friends.

The Eucharist remembers and re-enacts this sacrificial love that Jesus had for everyone.

Sacrifice is about choosing to think about others first.

Sacrifice is about spending time with others and not expecting anything in return.

In the Eucharist, the whole mystery of this is summed up in what is called the "mystery of faith": "Lord, by your cross and resurrection you have set us free, you are the Saviour of the world".

All meals are in some way sacrificial because time and energy and love go into them as well as the ingredients!

Extension work

A

Read John 21: 1–12 "Come and have breakfast". Put yourself in the picture. *Imagine* you are on the shore. *Explore* your thoughts and feelings.

B

On any journey, food is needed to sustain the travellers, and companionship or company can make a journey pass more quickly.

In what ways is the Christian's life like a journey?

In this country it is relatively easy to attend a Eucharist. *Find out* about the journeys some Christians have to make in order to take part in the Eucharist, for example in parts of Asia/Latin America/Africa.

The Eucharist – sign of peace

Task 28

Do you know how the handshake originated?
It was a symbolic gesture of peace. To use your right hand to take the right hand of another person proved that you carried no weapons with which to injure the other person.

Reflect on some of the arguments you may have got into when you were younger and not as mature as you are now. How was disagreement resolved? A handshake? Write about it or if you wish talk about it.

The Eucharist is not an escape from life: the food of the Eucharist strengthens people to go and transform the world by their ability to love and forgive others, and build a more just and peaceful world.

In South Africa many Catholics who are commited to working for justice are strengthened in the celebration of the Eucharist.

Why do you think this is so?

In the Eucharist, the sign of peace is a symbol of the unity of the community which has gathered together. The sign of peace is also a sign that the community will work for peace in the world.

There is peace with one another and with God: at the end of the Eucharist the Dismissal repeats this idea and there is another blessing:

> The Mass is ended, go in peace to love and serve the Lord.

When the Mass has ended, it has really just begun . . . The Christian is given the power to live the selfless way that Jesus lived and died on the Cross.

The Cross is the sign of peace. The mystery is that new life and new hope comes out of what looks like death and failure.

On the Cross, Jesus showed how much love God has for everyone, especially the poor.

In the Eucharist, Roman Catholics believe that Jesus is truly present in the consecrated bread and wine. They remember Jesus's words, "I will be with you".

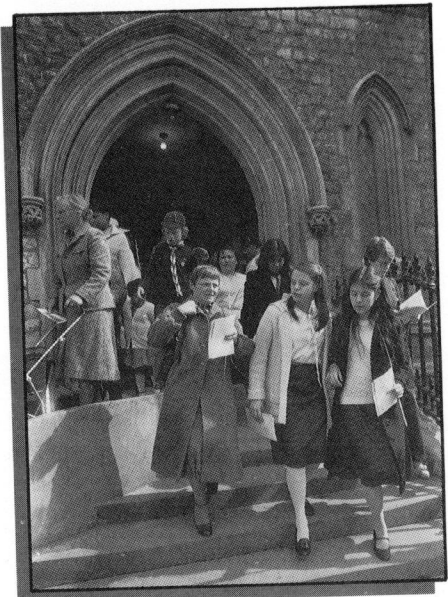

Extension work

A
Look at the Dismissal at the end of Mass and say what it means for you.

B
Compose a Dismissal which would be appropriate for the end of the Eucharist in:

- A parish near here.
- A township in South Africa.
- Or any other situation you wish to choose.

ASSESS your work!

How did we do?

Tasks 22–28

In what ways is the Mass a meal?
In what ways is the Mass a sacrifice?
Why is it important to celebrate the Eucharist?
What are Roman Catholics doing when the Eucharist is celebrated?

Review of the Module

Describe which part of the module you enjoyed most.
Look through your workbook and choose the best work.
What have you learned?
What did you find difficult?

We are the Champions!

Managing your own learning

Were you

1. Usually on time for class/usually late for class?
2. Hardworking . . . most of the time/some of the time/not very often?
3. Able to work by yourself sometimes?
4. Able to work with others in a group?

Did you

5. Find the work very easy or very difficult?
6. Work when the teacher was busy with other people or only when the teacher was with you?
7. Cooperate with the teacher?
8. Did you follow up any of the work you did at home by reading or finding out more about any of the topics you have covered?
9. Did you do any extension/project work?

Do you

10. Find it easy to tell the teacher of any problems you had?
11. Prefer to work by yourself or with others?

Now, share what you have done with your class teacher.

Congratulations!
You have now completed *Communication* Level Three.

This module in your R.E. programme is called

Celebration *Level Three*

In this module you will be reflecting on how people celebrate the mystery of life and death, particularly in Christianity and Islam, and how they celebrate the hope of overcoming pain and suffering.

Here are some of the things you will be doing in this module:

- **reflecting** on pain and suffering.

- **thinking about** the suffering experienced by some elderly and terminally-ill people.

- **finding out** about agencies locally and in the Third World who care for people who are sick or dying.

- **considering** what healing involves.

- **learning about** the Roman Catholic sacrament of the sick.

- **learning about** how the burial of the dead is celebrated in Christianity and Islam.

- **reflecting** on belief in life after death in Christianity and Islam.

- **reflecting** on the suffering and death of Jesus.

- **exploring** the symbols in the Easter celebration and the significance of Lent.

RECALL

If you have already studied the Level One and Level Two modules on Celebration, you should be able to recall the work you did.

Can you *remember*:

Level One:

- **describing** your experience of celebrations and special occasions?

- **exploring** some religious celebrations and festivals in Christianity and Hinduism?

Level Two
- **learning** about how people celebrate being set free?

- **analysing** Jewish and Christian celebrations of being set free?

Look back over your work in those modules and at your review of them. What do you think was your best work? What sort of activities did you get involved in? What did you learn from your study of these modules?

If this is your first Celebration module, remember that there are four strands of experience in this programme and that you will be reflecting on how people celebrate the mystery of life and death in each of the four contexts of:

home and family

local community

plural community

global community

The experience of pain and suffering

Task 1

Study the photographs below and try to imagine what the people involved are feeling.

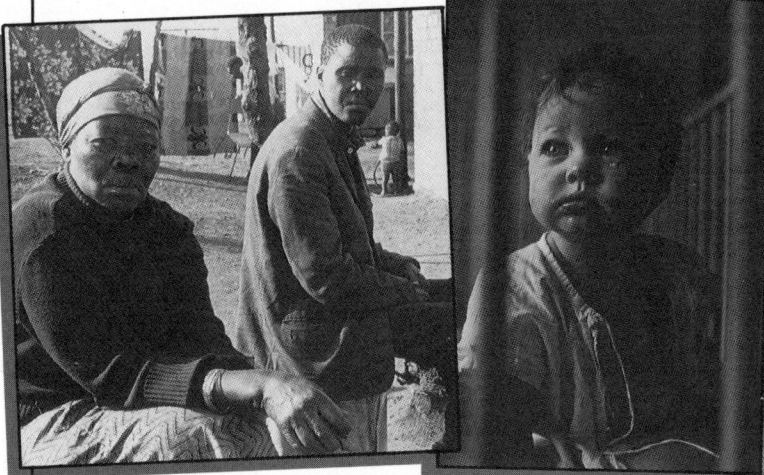

Use your imagination *to put yourself in the situation of the person at the centre of each of these scenes.*

Tell the story *of the central figures in these photographs in writing or on tape.*

Extension work

A

Find a way of expressing and communicating the mood of these pictures without using words – through movements or dance, perhaps.

B

Reflect – how do you feel as you look at these photographs? If you were at the scene, what would you think; feel; say; do?

What is your response when you see someone in pain or suffering?

Reflecting on your own experience of pain or suffering

Task 2

With your partner, think of some examples of painful experiences you may have had. For example:

- A time when you experienced a sharp physical pain.
- A time when you felt very ill.
- A time when you had your feelings hurt.
- A time when you felt great disappointment.
- A time of being anxious and worried.
- A time when you were victimised or worried.
- A time when you grieved for the death of someone you were close to.

Remember, some experiences may be too painful, personal or private to be discussed openly, but there are probably some examples you can think of that you can discuss comfortably.

For each example, **write down** a sentence or two only, and **pool** and **display** what your class has written.

Analyse your experiences.

Of the examples you have displayed: **Which** *relate to the pain or suffering people experience at home in their family life?*

Which *relate to the fact that there are different groups in the community between whom there are some tensions?*

Re-arrange the display so that these experiences are clustered together.

Reflect

Reflect *How much of this pain and suffering do you think is avoidable if certain things were done or certain decisions were made?*

Extension work

A

Reflect – how did you deal with your pain or hurt in the examples you thought of?

Who helped or supported you at that time?

B

Which kinds of pain and suffering are most difficult to think about and talk about?

Write a poem or short story about one of the experiences you have had from the list above.

Life without pain

FACT

There have been a few recorded cases in medical history in Britain of people who have been unable to feel any kind of physical pain – no twinges, no headaches or toothache, no feeling of being bruised or cut, no pains to warn you that something is wrong inside or that what you are touching is dangerously hot.

Task 3

With your partner, discuss what would be good and what would be bad about having no sense of pain.

Then, consider whether some kinds of pain may have a purpose and be a useful thing even if very unpleasant.

Decide whether there are any kinds of pain which you consider useless.

Extension work

A

Design a sequence of movements to illustrate (give a picture of) certain types of pain.

B

Reflect: do you think it is possible for a person to go through life without any pain or suffering at all?

Charting pain and suffering

Some pain is –
physical . . . hitting your thumb with a hammer.

Some pain is –
mental . . . suffering terrible worries.

Sometimes it is –
both, e.g. being anxious about an illness.

Some suffering is –
natural, an inevitable part of being alive in the world, e.g. grief at the death of a parent.

Some suffering is –
caused by people, e.g. mugging.

Task 4 GROUP WORK

Brainstorm in your group at least ten examples of pain and suffering, or choose them from the list of experiences in Task 2 and list them in the left *hand column of the chart which you have copied into your file or workbook. Then analyse which descriptions fit your example and tick the column.*

Examples	Physical	Mental	Physical and Mental	Natural	Caused by other People	Caused by Self
1.						
2.						
3.						

Extension work

A

Pain and suffering.
These words all came from one newspaper on one day.

Can you find any similar examples of headlines and stories about pain, suffering and tragedy in a recent newspaper?

Display them.

TRAGEDY **CRISIS**
worries
hurt and sorrow
Hard times
stress **upsets**
bereavement

B

Analyse news reports in the papers or on TV. How much of the news involves reports about the kind of things in the headlines above?

Pick one newspaper or one bulletin of the news. Now analyse what you read or hear in the news. What proportion of the paper or news bulletin deals with pain or suffering?

Reflect: why is so much of the news to do with pain, suffering and strife?

Pandora's box

Task 5

For centuries people have asked the question
"Why is there pain and suffering?"

Prometheus, a fire-god who was given to playing tricks on the other gods, had given the gift of fire to mortals without the consent of the others. Zeus, the king of the gods, determined to counteract this blessing, so he got Hephaestus, the patron of craftsmen, to fashion a woman, Pandora, to whom the gods gave various gifts. She had a box containing all sorts of evil and misery and suffering. Zeus sent her to Epimetheus who married her. Everyone was curious as to what the box contained but she had been warned on no account to open the box. Eventually she could resist no longer and lifted the lid of the box, at which evil and misery and suffering escaped and flew all over the earth. Pandora slammed the lid down, and the one thing that was left inside the box, Hope, was firmly locked inside.

Discuss: What did the people who told this story believe about the origins of evil and suffering in the world?

Recall the stories of Creation in Genesis Chapter 1 and 2.
What do they say about good and evil in the world?

Read the story of the Tower of Babel in Genesis 11:1–9.
What does it see as the cause of the chaos and division among people?

Extension work

A

Express, communicate one of these stories in actions, music, dance, or visually on a display board.

or

Write your own story about the beginning of pain and suffering, and the possibility of hope.

B

Reflect and *evaluate:* what are these stories saying about pain and suffering?
What do you think?

Response to accidents and natural disasters

Task 6

Look at the selection of newspaper stories below. With your partner, recall what you know or have heard about these tragedies.

Can you think of any significant events which have happened recently which you might want to add to this catalogue of disasters?

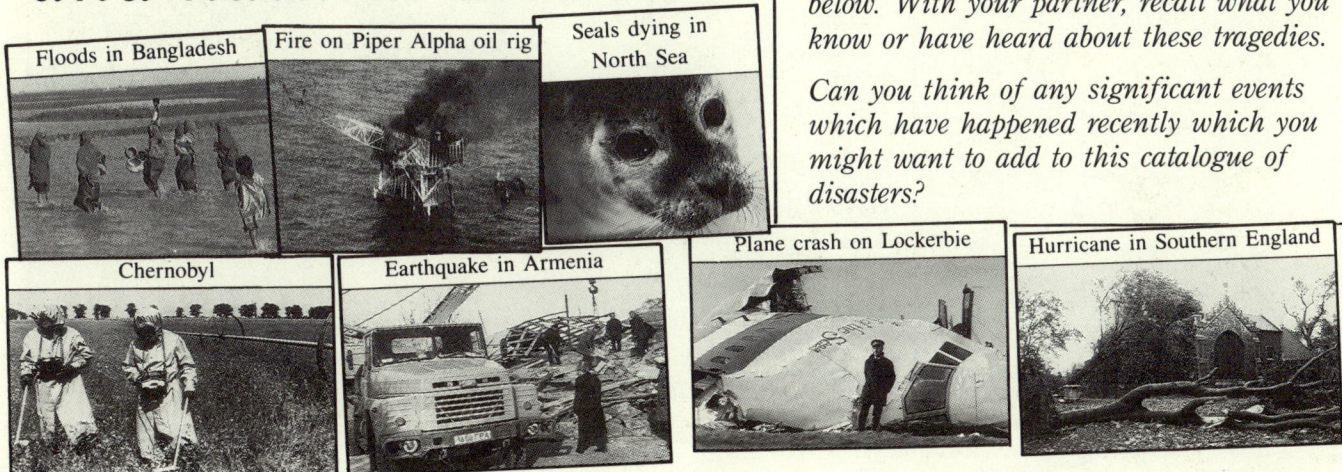

Floods in Bangladesh

Fire on Piper Alpha oil rig

Seals dying in North Sea

Chernobyl

Earthquake in Armenia

Plane crash on Lockerbie

Hurricane in Southern England

GROUP WORK

Take each example and discuss the following questions for each one:

1. *What was the reaction of people who survived or witnessed the event?*

2. *What has been done to make sure that those who lost their lives or face a life of pain and suffering are not quickly forgotten? What ceremonies have taken place, if any, to mark the importance of what happened?*

3. *Has the incident or accident prompted people to try to guard against this happening again?*

4. *Which of these tragedies was potentially avoidable?*

   How much can be put down to human error or negligence?

   How much to uncontrollable forces of nature?

5. *What gives some people hope to recover and strength to carry on living after a tragedy?*

Reflection

Considering all the examples together, how might people who believe that there is a God who is good and cares for his creatures and all creation explain the fact that there is a great deal of pain and suffering in the world, some of it caused by events of nature such as earthquakes and volcanoes?

Extension work

A

Reflect: Imagine you had been involved in, witnessed or survived one of the disasters mentioned at the start of this task.

What would you have felt?

What questions do you think you might have asked?

Do you think your view of life would be altered in any way? If so, how?

B

Research and *reflect: Find out* about how people in your area respond to the needs of those whose lives have been affected by tragedy.

What do local churches and other religious groups do?

What organisations are there and how do they motivate people to get involved?

Have you ever played a part in responding to a need like this?

ASSESS your work!

How did we do?

Tasks 1–6

1. *How well did you empathise with (try to imagine the feelings of) the people in the photographs in Task 1?*

2. *Did you find it easy or difficult to recall your own experience of pain or hurt?*

3. *Did you explore this early part of the module through movements and dance, at all?*

4. *How do you respond to the news of disasters? Does it make you think? Or feel certain emotions?*

5. *How much extension work have you managed?*

Old age

Task 7

An individual or class project

Analyse *the part which pain and illness and lack of mobility play in the lives of the elderly.*

Research *the opportunities and difficulties faced by the elderly in your local community:*

- *By pooling what each of you in your class knows.*
- *By inviting in the district nurse or a social worker or a member of a voluntary organisation such as "meals on wheels" or an organiser of a club for retired or elderly people.*
- *By visiting someone who lives near you and who faces these difficulties.*

Plan *how you will approach the task, especially if you invite a speaker or go to visit an elderly person. You will realise that this task needs to be approached sensitively.*

Choose *a method of recording what you have found out about the part which pain and suffering plays in the life of the elderly in your locality.*

Reflect *on their situation.*

How is old age celebrated in your community?

George van Dewson, aged 83 had his record "It's party time again" re-released 50 years on, and it made the pop charts.

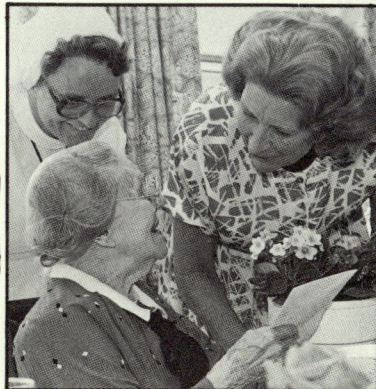

Every year the Queen sends telegrams to elderly people who have reached their 100th birthday.

Hundreds of pensioners recently lobbied the Prime Minister about possible plans to reduce State pensions.

Extension work

A

Write a pen-picture of an elderly person in your community that you admire.

or

Record an interview with an elderly person that you know. Plan some of the questions that you might want to ask.

B GROUP WORK

Prepare a presentation of your work on this task for Assembly.

Consider:

- How you will gain the interest of people at the Assembly.
- What visual material you can use to make the presentation effective.
- How each of you will be involved.
- What you will be asking the Assembly to do, e.g. reflect, see, listen.

A global view

When people are very old and near to death they need special care and support from those around them. In fact all those who are terminally ill need not just medical help but to feel that they can face death with dignity and with the support of compassionate people.

The story is told that one day Mother Teresa was walking in the streets of Calcutta, when she heard a very weak, distressed voice speaking from somewhere in a back alleyway. She went to look and found a very frail and starved old lady crumpled into a box. She lifted her into her arms and carried her back to the hospice which she runs for the elderly, sick and dying in Calcutta. On the way, the old lady murmured,

66 My son did this to me. 99

Task 8

Explore the work of the Sisters in the communities founded by Mother Teresa. Their hospices for the sick and dying are in many countries, including India and Britain.

Extension work

A

Prepare a Fact File on the work of an organisation which helps the elderly locally or overseas (e.g. Help the Aged, Hospices, etc).

Wherever you look in the world people who are dying from disease or from old age need the support of the community. This is true in India and in Africa, in China and in Britain.

Two days later, in her bed at the hospice, the old lady died, holding the hand of one of the sisters. Despite her terrible experience, she died peacefully and happily. The last words she said were

66 I have lived my life with no more than the dogs have, but now I am going to die like an angel. 99

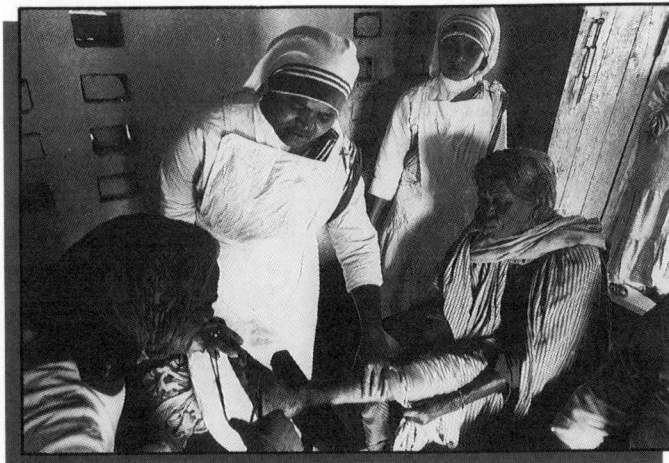

B

Invite someone from an organisation which helps the sick and elderly to speak to your class.

ASSESS your work!

How did we do?

Tasks 7—8

1. *What did you learn about the opportunities and difficulties associated with old age?*
2. *What did you discover about the experience of being an elderly person in your community?*
3. *How would you evaluate the work done by Mother Teresa and her sisters in their hospices?*
4. *Did you particularly enjoy doing any part of these two tasks?*

Suffering in Islam

The word Islam means resignation or submission to the will of Allah.

Task 9

Read this passage from the Qur'ān. What does it say?

Explain this passage, in your own words, to your partner.

> Say:
> O God of Kings you give authority to whom you will and you remove authority from whom you will, you exalt whom you will and you diminish whom you will. In your hand all is good, truly you have power over every single thing.
> To God belongs everything in the heavens and in the earth; he forgives whom he wills, he punishes whom he wills, and God is forgiving, compassionate.
>
> Surah 3

Extension work

A

Muslims see suffering as a way that God

● punishes for wrongdoing

● puts people to the test

The response to personal suffering is to accept the will of God.

Discuss and *record* your view of suffering.

B

All Muslims are required to give alms so that poverty and injustice be removed from society . . . so action is an important response to the suffering of others.

What do you think? *Reflect* and then *evaluate* the two approaches to suffering – accepting and acting.

Fasting in Islam (saum)
the festival of Ramadan

Islam means "submission" or "complete obedience" to the will of Allah, and involves five basic duties (the five "pillars" of Islam). The first involves declaring one's belief in Allah as revealed through the prophet Muhammad. The other duties are ways of living out this belief in practice, and in this module you will be looking at how Muslims celebrate their belief in God in two of the "pillars" or duties – fasting and pilgrimage.

INFORMATION

Ramadan is the ninth month of the Muslim calendar and is sacred to Muslims because they believe that it was during this month that the Qur'ān was revealed to Muhammad on the Night of Power. (See Level Three, Story module.) The Qur'ān prescribes that fasting should take place in the month of Ramadan.

WORK IT OUT

The Muslim calendar dates from the year 622 when Muhammad went from Mecca to Medina – a journey called the Hijrah. A Muslim year is based on the lunar calendar, which is 11 days (12 in a leap year) shorter than the solar year. So to convert from AD (*anno domini*) to AH (after Hijrah), use the formula

$$AD = AH + 622 - \frac{AH}{32}$$

$$AH = AD - 622 + \frac{AD - 622}{32}$$

So 1987 AD = 1407 AH

Can you find out from this what the present year AD is in the Muslim calendar?

ISMAIL'S STORY

Hello! My name's Ismail. I'm 18 and I work in a textile factory in Rochdale. I'm going to tell you about how my community observes the command to worship through fasting, which we call saum, the fourth pillar of Islam. The Qur'ān tells us "You who believe! Fasting is prescribed for you just as it was prescribed for those before you, so that you may ward off evil" (Surah 2).

When we fast it is not just a matter of not eating and drinking during the hours of daylight. It is a way of responding to God spiritually, in obedience and by strict self-discipline for a long period of time – a whole month!

During that time, devout Muslims refrain from eating, drinking and sexual relations during the hours of daylight between dawn and sunset. Young children, the sick, the elderly and women who are pregnant are all excused from fasting but they are encouraged to do **some** fasting during this time. It is very hard when you are at work and other people are going off to have snacks and lunchbreaks but, of course, fasting isn't meant to be easy. When I get home from work, and it starts to get dark, I usually have a light snack with my family and then a bit later, we say our night prayers (Maghrib) and have a full meal. Before dawn we have another meal before starting to fast again. When Ramadan falls in the winter the fasting is for a shorter day; when it falls in the summer, there are much longer hours of daylight.

Because this is a spiritual, religious experience, I must be even more careful during Ramadan to be truthful and not to break a promise, get angry or speak badly of others. It is also a prayerful time and we are expected to say more prayers than usual during Ramadan.

I think there are really three great benefits that fasting can bring. First, by fasting and self-discipline you can be freed from your desires and habits and turn to Allah, who is the supporter and sustainer of all life. Second, you identify with people who are hungry and suffering, and you feel some sympathy for the poor and those who do not have the comforts you normally have. Third, you know that Muslims all over the world are fasting with you, and you are aware of being part of a community and that after the fast, you and your community will be spiritually enriched and encouraged for a life of submission to the will of God.

Task 10

Describe the kind of training and discipline that a top athlete like Florence Griffiths Joyner or Daley Thompson has to undergo. Can you think of any other walks of life where this might be necessary?

Does everyone's life need discipline?

Why do you think people diet?

Analyse: *why are discipline and self control vital for the people you have been describing?*

Reflect: *are you involved in any difficult or painful experiences in order to achieve a goal or ambition of some kind?*

Extension work

A

Make a summary of what Ismail feels he gains from fasting and penance during Ramadan.

B

Reflect: this module is called *Celebration.* Why do you think you might be considering pain, suffering, fasting and penance as part of a unit on celebration?

The festival of Eid-ul-Fitr

the end of Ramadan

Ismail's sister, Rahila, is still at school. Here she tells us about the festival of Eid-ul-Fitr which comes at the end of Ramadan.

I always look forward to Eid-ul-Fitr. It happens on the first day of the next month after Ramadan, the month of Shawal. This is the festival of fast-breaking, a very happy time full of thanksgiving and rejoicing for the help which Allah gives to us for the month of fasting. On the first day of Eid, everyone in our house gets up and has a bath or shower before dressing up in their very best clothes or even new clothes bought for the festival. We go to the mosque to pray and then we visit our relations and friends. I always get Eid cards from my friends and I decorate our living-room with them, and people give each other presents – my relatives usually give me some money so that I can save up to buy what I want. Usually at midday on the first day of Eid, we sit down and share the first midday meal for a month. I always say a little prayer for my grandfather on that day because Muslims remember their dead relatives during the Eid festival and sometimes visit their graves. The festival is also a time for giving Zakat – money for the poor.

Task 11

Can you show how the festivals of Ramadan and Eid-ul-Fitr give an opportunity for Muslims to fulfil at least four of the five "pillars" of Islam?

Reminder:
The five pillars of Islam
Shahadah – declaring faith.
Salat – prayer.
Zakat – giving to the poor.
Saum – fasting.
Hajj – pilgrimage.

Extension work

A

Reflect: why do Muslims celebrate the festival of Eid-ul-Fitr?

B

Research or *Recall:* What part does fasting and self-discipline play in Hinduism and Buddhism?

Pilgrimage (hajj)

the fifth pillar of Islam, and Eid-ul Adha

Every Muslim is required, if it is at all possible, once in their lifetime to make a pilgrimage to Mecca. Rahila had found her grandfather's diary from when he made the hajj – the pilgrimage to Mecca. Here are some extracts from it:

TUESDAY

We went into the courtyard where the Ka'aba is, and walked around it seven times. There were huge crowds but everyone was patient and made way for others. I was determined, like all Muslims, to try and touch or kiss the Black Stone, and I thanked Allah when I was eventually able to work my way to the middle of the courtyard and do this. We joined in with the prayers being recited in happiness and thanksgiving. It was a life's ambition realised.

Later on we made for the hills of Safa and Marwah, walking between them and remembering the story of Abraham's wife, Hagar, going looking for water. We refreshed ourselves with a drink from the well, and I filled a little bottle with the water to bring back home to the family.

TUESDAY (ninth day of the pilgrimage)

We travelled to Arafat, a short way from Mecca, and prayed with all the other thousands of pilgrims, and stayed in the tents there until sunset. I felt very much part of a worldwide brotherhood of different nationalities and attitudes. After sunset, we visited Mina where Abraham was tempted by the devil not to do the will of Allah – and we threw stones at the three pillars there to show we rejected evil.

We celebrated the feast of sacrifice, Eid-ul-Adha, where an animal is sacrificed and the meat is given to the poor. Like the hajj itself, the festival reminds Muslims that they should be prepared like Abraham, to sacrifice everything for Allah.

MONDAY (first day of pilgrimage)

Our plane landed at Jeddah and we travelled on in the Arabian heat to Mecca, the birthplace of Muhammad and the city which houses the Ka'aba, which we Muslims believe to have been built by Abraham, and towards which we turn when praying.

Before entering the city, we put on the simple white garments of ihram which all the pilgrims wear. It is a sign of sacrificing all your possessions and putting aside your worldly achievements and status, and all being equally pilgrims and servants of Allah. It is also a sign of getting yourself into the right frame of mind and spiritual readiness for the pilgrimage.

THURSDAY

I went to the barber's and had my head shaved, just like when I was a baby. This reminds us that we are starting a new life. We walked around the Ka'aba again and that was the end of hajj and the need to wear ihram.

MONDAY

Arrived back home to a great welcome from the family – it took all day to tell the story!

Task 12

Knowledge: *what are the duties which a Muslim performs as part of the hajj?*

Understanding: *how is the hajj seen as a way of celebrating obedience to Allah?*

Evaluation: *what does the hajj tell you about the commitment of Muslims to follow Allah?*

Extension work

A

Reflect: have you ever had to make some sacrifices in order to achieve an aim? Describe what that was like.

B

Research: Explore the life and beliefs of someone who made the sacrifice of giving their own life for the sake of their religious beliefs. Do you find their story unsettling, challenging or inspiring?

A Muslim funeral

An extract from the diary of Abdul Ghulam Khan, aged 14, who lives in Wolverhampton.

June 5th

I knew something was wrong when I got home from school and found my sister, Surriya, crying in the kitchen. I ran upstairs to my grandfather's bedroom (he has been very ill for a long time now) and found my father and mother and my uncle Muzzamil at grandad's bedside. My grandad was speaking very softly – 'La ilaha illallah Muhammadu rasulullah' – that's Arabic and it's the special prayer called the Kalimah which expresses our Muslim faith. It says 'There is no God but Allah and Muhammad is Allah's messenger.'

He died peacefully soon after that and we all said the prayer – 'We belong to Allah and to him we shall return'. Shortly afterwards the undertaker came and arranged for grandad's body to be taken to the mosque for the funeral preparations.

It was a very sad night in our house.

June 10th

This morning I went to the mosque for the funeral. It is our custom that only the men in the family attend funerals. On the way my father explained that the body had been carefully washed and then wrapped in a white garment and Ifthikhar's (that was grandad's name) head was turned to face to the right. Then the coffin was placed in a special room in the mosque with the body lying in such a way that the head faced towards Mecca. Grandad had been on pilgrimage (Hajj) to Mecca before he got ill, and the white garment he wore then was the one he had been wrapped in for his funeral. When we arrived the Imam started the special funeral prayer (the Salat al Janazah) which starts 'Allahu Akbar' meaning God is the greatest.

There was a reading from the Quran and then more prayers and the peace greeting 'Peace be upon you and the mercy of Allah'.

The Imam said lots of nice things about how Ifthikhar will be remembered in his children and his good example and in what he leaves behind for the future care of his family. Grandad didn't have a lot of money but he died knowing that his family had all they needed for a happy life. He was buried in the local cemetery like all Muslims (we don't have cremations) with his head to the south west end of the grave and still facing Mecca.

Task 13

Read Ghulam's diary.

Compare and contrast this account with any funeral you have seen or attended.

GROUP WORK

Make a list of questions you would like the class to be able to discuss with your teacher.

Extension work

A

Visit your local cemetery and observe how the memory of the dead is celebrated.

B

How is the memory of the dead celebrated in other ways in your community?

Tasks 9–13

1. *What is the attitude of Muslims to pain and suffering?*
2. *Why is fasting important to Muslims?*
3. *Can you see any connection between everyday discipline and self-control and responses to pain and suffering?*
4. *What have you learned about the differences between dieting to lose weight, discipline for athletic training, and fasting for religious reasons?*
5. *What are the points of similarity between fasting in the Christian way of life and in the Islamic way of life?*
6. *What did you learn about Eid-ul-Fitr?*
7. *What Islamic beliefs are involved in the completion of the hajj?*
8. *What do you recall about the funeral of Abdul's grandfather?*
9. *Did you find this part of the module interesting?*

Suffering in the Old Testament

For Jews and Christians the Old Testament deals with many aspects and approaches to suffering.

Task 14

Read Jeremiah 7:1–11

Role-play a situation where someone is trying to persuade others that their country is about to be invaded unless they do something about it. They take no notice and eventually the enemy invades and a lot of suffering follows. Only then do they realise that they should have listened to Jeremiah.

Extension work

A

"Sometimes people do not realise how happy or free or healthy they are until all that is taken away from them. Sometimes when people experience suffering they realise how wrong they have been about what life means and what they have lost."

Compose some brief dramatic scenes to illustrate these points.

B

Jeremiah criticised those who worshipped God outwardly but not in their hearts nor in their everyday lives. He became very unpopular because of this.

Reflect do you know of anyone who suffered because he/she spoke an unpopular truth?

Healing in the New Testament

Task 15

Analyse: *What was Jesus' response to pain and suffering?*
You will find different groups of people in the gospels whom Jesus met, cared for and cured.

| physical illness and disability | suffering from guilt, worry, confusion, etc. | possessed and mentally ill |

restoring to life

Can you find some examples of each of these?

For each example, check which of these applies to the response of Jesus to the person involved.

1. *He listened to them.*   4. *He comforted and strengthened them.*
2. *He felt sorry for them.*   5. *He healed them.*
3. *He forgave them.*   6. *He restored them to life.*

Extension work

A

Act out in mime (without words) one of the gospel stories you have read about healing.

B

Can you *find out* about any Christian groups in your area that dedicate themselves to caring for the sick?

The sacrament of the sick in the Roman Catholic church

An interview with Father John, parish priest

Susan: Thank you for agreeing to be interviewed, Father. We're interested in what your church community does for those who are sick or near to death.

Father John: Well, as you might imagine, this is a difficult area of parish life, because sickness, suffering and dying are so hard to come to terms with. But we do have a number of ways in which we try to help people. You must remember that we believe that God loves his people and wants them to be happy with him forever. He sent his Son, Jesus, to show us what God's love is like, and so we model ourselves on Jesus who comforted the sick and healed them; made them whole again.

James: What do you actually do?

Father John: In the first place, we pray for those who are sick and dying. In most of our services and in private prayer and worship, we always try to remember those in need and we ask that God will give them strength and courage.

Susan: Do you expect that they will always recover?

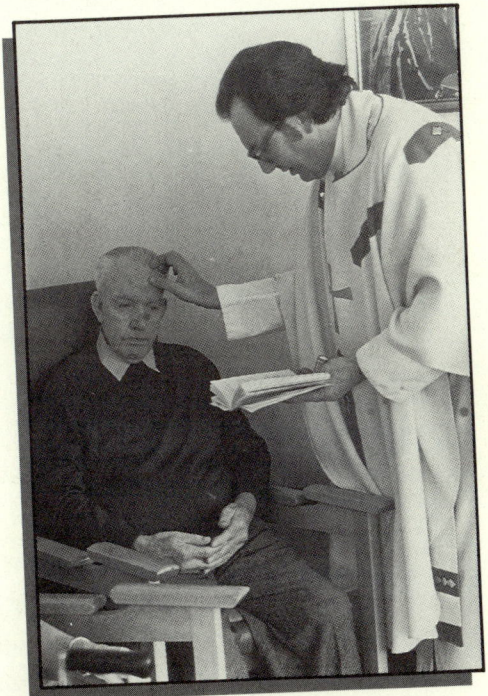

Father John: We pray that God will give people the strength to be able to respond to whatever he will ask of them. I am sure that sometimes people get better, helped by our prayers and the care and time that we give to them. Sometimes God seems to be asking us to be with a person as they prepare to die and come to see God in the fullest way.

James: Is it just prayer?

Father John: In one way, yes – everything we do for God is prayer. But I know what you mean. It isn't just prayer in church. For example, when our community celebrates the Eucharist, we have lay ministers, people in the parish, who have a special task of giving people communion during Mass and taking communion to people at home who are too sick to come to church. Once a month, I do the same for all the very old, housebound or sick people in my parish. We Catholics believe that the bread and wine at Mass become the body and blood of Jesus – so when they receive communion, Jesus is really coming to be with them.

Susan: What is the "sacrament of the sick?"

Father John: Well, that is a special ceremony when someone is particularly ill or possibly near to death. Friends and relatives gather at the sick person's bedside, and a table is set with a crucifix, candles, some holy water and a small container with holy oil in it. A passage is read from the Bible and some prayers are said for the sick person. Then I anoint the sick person with oil – a symbol of God's strength being given to the person. Usually the sacrament ends with the person who is sick being blessed and receiving Holy Communion, and of course, encouragement from those present.

James: Where does this practice come from?

Father John: Well actually, from Jesus and the early church, and it's mentioned in a letter by your namesake, James. You can look it up when you get back to school.

Susan: Thank you, Father John. It's time we did just that!

Task 16

Look up *the Letter of James 5:14–16.*

Compare *what you read there with Father John's account of the sacrament of the sick.*

Write down *the similarities.*

Word work: all the following words have been used in this task:

sacrament	symbol	lay minister	Eucharist
crucifix	anoint	Holy Communion	sacrament of the sick

Discuss with your partner what each word means and write the meaning down.

Find a way of checking your work.

Extension work

A

Reflect: have you ever spent any time with a person who was rather ill? What did you do and say? *Describe* how you felt.

Why do people pray for the sick?

What do you **think** about this?

B

Research: Find out what is done in a local Christian church or parish for those who are sick or near to death.

Pilgrimage in Christianity

Catherine's visit to Lourdes

Catherine is 13 and was born spina bifida. She is confined to a wheelchair and at the moment attends a special school which has the facilities she needs. Her family and friends have been saving up and organising money-raising events to enable her to go to Lourdes on a pilgrimage. When she goes she will travel on a specially-constructed coach so that the journey will not be as difficult as it would be on public transport. She will have a special friend and helper, Colette, who is a student at college. Colette will look after Catherine for the whole trip. She will, of course, be with lots of other young people making the same pilgrimage. It is a special journey for Catherine because she will make lots of new friends and experience the love and care of this small community as it travels to and from the shrine of Lourdes. She is looking forward to her visit to the grotto of Our Lady where St. Bernadette experienced visions of Mary, the Mother of Jesus, in 1858. There are baths where the sick and most visitors are bathed. People pray that Mary will ask God's blessing and healing for them. Many people have returned from Lourdes cured of their illnesses. Most pilgrims are happy to go and pray and return home spiritually enriched and with their lives changed in some way, even if they have not been physically healed. There is a special torchlight procession of the pilgrims which celebrates their faith in Jesus as the one who brings light into a world darkened by pain and suffering.

Task 17

Imagine that you are Catherine and describe the experience of going on the pilgrimage.

Extension work

A

What do you think is the value of a pilgrimage to Lourdes for those who are sick and for those who are in good health?

Do you know of any other places of pilgrimage in this country or abroad?

B

Do you know anyone who has been to Lourdes or another place of pilgrimage? *Ask* them about the experience, *write* it up in your file and *share* it with the class or invite them to speak to your class.

The suffering and death of Jesus

Task 18

Read the account of Jesus' trial and crucifixion in the gospel of Luke 22:39–23:56, or listen to a tape of it being read or acted out. Make your own tape.

Put yourself in the position of the people involved and try to imagine what they would have been thinking and what they would have felt.

| The Roman soldiers | Pilate | Jesus' disciples and friends |

| Jesus himself | Judas | The crowd | Peter |

For Christians, the *Cross* is a symbol of the suffering and death of Jesus. Christians believe that Jesus suffered and died and rose from the dead so that all people might be saved, might have hope of overcoming failure, evil and suffering in life and come close to God for ever; Jesus' body was broken and killed so that others might be made whole; Jesus died so that all people might have eternal life.

Another way in which Christian faith in Jesus can be expressed is this:

Jesus was fully *human*. He experienced pain, suffering and death, and identified with all who suffer and die.

Jesus was fully *divine*. He overcame suffering and death and made it possible for all people of good will to share everlasting life.

Here are some images of the crucifixion in art:

Reflect: *which of these do you think best expresses and communicates what Jesus' suffering and death mean for Christians today?*

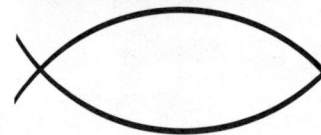

Extension work

A

What feelings are mentioned in the crucifixion account that you read at the beginning of this task? *Explore* some movements and shapes to express these.

B

Reflect: some recent films depicting the life of Jesus have ended with his death and burial. Why would you think Christians might argue that this does not reflect Christian belief and teaching about Jesus?

ICHTHUS

= J(esus)
= CH(rist)
= TH(eou) (of God)
= U(ios) (Son)
= S(aviour)

The Christian celebration of Easter

Easter Sunday is the most important day in the Christian calendar because it is the day when Christians celebrate their belief in Jesus, risen from the dead.

Remember: the gospels were written by the followers of Jesus, who believed that he was risen from the dead. They record the belief of the Christian community in Jesus, the Son of God, risen from the dead and saviour of the world. One of the first symbols of the Christian church was a fish – the Greek word for fish was the first letters of the words Jesus Christ Son of God Saviour. (See p. 46)

Task 19

Examine the evidence. Read Matthew 27:55–28:20.

Prepare a statement from the witnesses:

- Mary Magdalene and her friends found the tomb empty. (See John 20:1–18.)
- Two disciples on the road to Emmaus. (See Luke 24:13–32.)
- The Eleven Apostles. (See Luke 24:33–53.)
- Five-hundred followers. (See Paul's letter 1 Cor. 15:1–8.)

On Easter night, the Saturday before Easter Sunday, Roman Catholics celebrate the Easter Vigil Mass in which a number of symbols are used. At the beginning of the Easter Vigil the priest welcomes the people with words like these:

> 66 Dear friends in Christ,
> on this most holy night,
> when our Lord Jesus
>   Christ passed from
>   death to life,
> the Church invites her
>   children throughout the
>   world
> to come together in vigil
>   and prayer.
> This is the passover of
>   the Lord. 99

Symbols and prayers

> 66 Father,
> we share in the light of your glory
> through your Son, the light of the world.
> Make this new fire holy and inflame us with new hope. 99

> 66 My brothers and sisters,
> let us ask the Lord our God
> to bless this water he has created,
> which we shall use to recall our baptism.
> May he renew us
> and keep us faithful to the Spirit
> we have all received. 99

> 66 May the light of Christ, rising in glory,
> dispel the darkness of our hearts and minds. 99

> 66 By his holy
> and glorious wounds
> may Christ our Lord
> guard us and keep us. 99

Extension work

A

Explore what the symbols and prayers express about the meaning of Easter for Catholics and other Christians.

B

There are many customs and traditions connected with Easter celebrations. *Find out* about some of these and *explore* how they relate to what people are celebrating (e.g. Easter eggs/Easter chicks).

Lent – preparation for Easter

For Christians Lent is a special time of preparation for Easter. For adults who are to be baptised and become members of the Roman Catholic Church at Easter it is the final weeks of their spiritual preparation.

The Latin word for Lent is *"quaresima"* which comes from the word for 40. In the gospels there are stories about Jesus spending 40 days in the wilderness as he prepared himself for his mission with the people. Christians commemorate this in the 40 days from Ash Wednesday to the Easter Vigil on Holy Saturday night. They often try to do something extra which demands some effort because it is not always easy, or they decide to do without something which they enjoy. Christians do this as a way of fasting and doing penance which helps self-discipline and control, recalls the suffering of Jesus, and prepares them to renew the promises they made at baptism during the celebration of Easter.

Task 20

Read the following Lenten prayers and list the things they suggest Christians should do during Lent. Why should Christians do these things?

Each year you give us this joyful season
when we prepare to celebrate the paschal
   mystery
with mind and heart renewed.
You give us a spirit of loving reverence for
   you, our Father,
and of willing service to our neighbour.
                (Lenten Preface I)

Turn away from sin and be faithful to the
   gospel.
        (Prayer on receiving the ashes)

God of all compassion, Father of all
   goodness,
to heal the wounds our sins and selfishness
   bring upon us
you bid us turn to fasting, prayer, and
   sharing with our brothers.
        (Prayer of 3rd Sunday of Lent)

Father in heaven,
the love of your Son led him to accept the
   suffering of the cross
that we might glory in new life.
Change our selfishness into self-giving.
Help us to embrace the world you have given
   us,
that we may transform the darkness of its pain
into the life and joy of Easter.
        (Prayer on 5th Sunday in Lent)

Extension work

A

Find out what is celebrated on these days – Shrove Tuesday, Ash Wednesday, Passion or Palm Sunday. For Roman Catholics Ash Wednesday and Good Friday are days of fasting and abstinence – what does that mean?

B

In many countries, especially in Europe and South America, the days just before Lent are known as carnival (from the Latin words meaning "goodbye meat"). *Explore* its origins and ways in which it is celebrated.

Having explored the Easter Faith of Christians, we examine its implications, for the Christian attitude to death.

A Christian funeral

Evening Post

De Silva, Anne, aged 74, loving wife of Paul, mother of Gina and Frank, and grandmother of Karen, Dean and James, after a long illness. Reception into St. Nicholas's Church, Tuesday evening, 7 p.m., Requiem Mass, Wed. 9.30 a.m., followed by interment at Longmoor Cemetery.

Karen linked her mum's arm as they went into church on Wednesday morning for gran's funeral. The coffin had been brought into church the night before and prayers had been said for Anne. Her death had been the end of a long and painful illness, and although her family were very sad at her death, it was something of a relief that her suffering was at an end. Father Tom had comforted Karen's parents, and was here now to take the funeral service. Requiem means *rest* or *peace* and comes from the prayer said several times at a funeral:

> "Eternal rest give to her, O Lord,
> and let perpetual light shine upon her.
> May she rest in peace, Amen."

Karen was very upset. She had been very close to gran, especially after grandad had died. Now she was missing her very much, but she was comforted by the knowledge that gran was now on her way to God. Father Tom summed it up in his sermon:

"We're here today to pray for Anne: may she be received into the life of God. We also thank God for Anne's life, for the love and friendship which she shared with us. We will always remember her. We are sad that our close relative and friend has died and we ask God for his support and strength in this time of mourning. And we are reminded today that we all will one day face death and judgement. We look forward with great hope, confident in our faith in Jesus who rose from the dead and has made it possible for us too to share eternal life with God our Father in heaven."

Karen was only too aware of all those feelings mixed together – sorrow and joy, loneliness and closeness, fear and hope for the future.

At the graveside the family gathered round as the coffin was lowered into the grave, and the mourners said the "Our Father" together. Karen was suddenly much more aware of another aspect of her Christian faith. She knew that in one way this was the end of gran's life, that her body was dead and now buried, but in another way, this was the beginning of life with God for ever. Christians believe that the soul of a person does not die but continues to live.

Some prayers from the funeral Mass:

"Merciful Father,
hear our prayers and console us.
As we renew our faith in your Son,
whom you raised from the dead,
strengthen our hope that all our departed brothers and sisters
will share in his resurrection,
who lives and reigns with you and the Holy Spirit,
one God, for ever and ever."
(from the Opening Prayer)

"We believe in one Lord, Jesus Christ,
the only Son of God,
eternally begotten of the Father,
God from God, Light from Light,
true God from true God . . .
For our sake he was crucified under Pontius Pilate;
 he suffered death and was buried.
On the third day he rose again
 in accordance with the Scriptures;
he ascended into heaven
 and is seated at the right hand of the Father.
He will come again in glory to judge the living and the dead,
 and his kingdom will have no end. . . .
We look for the resurrection of the dead,
 and the life of the world to come. Amen."
(from the Creed)

Task 21

Read the story about the funeral and the prayers from the Mass. Have you ever been to a funeral? What do the prayers tell you about the beliefs and hopes of the Christian community? Can you put these in your own words?

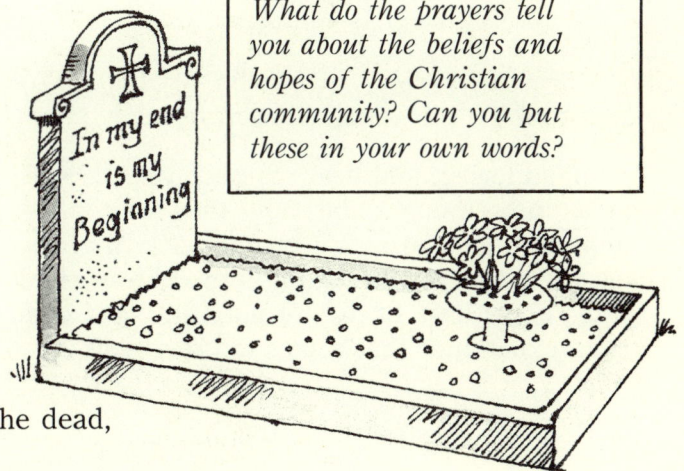

In my end is my Beginning

"Father, all-powerful and ever-living God,
we do well always and everywhere to give you thanks
through Jesus Christ our Lord.

In him, who rose from the dead,
our hope of resurrection dawned.
The sadness of death gives way
to the bright promise of immortality.

Lord, for your faithful people life is changed, not ended.

When the body of our earthly dwelling lies in death
we gain an everlasting dwelling place in heaven."

(from the Preface of Christian Death I)

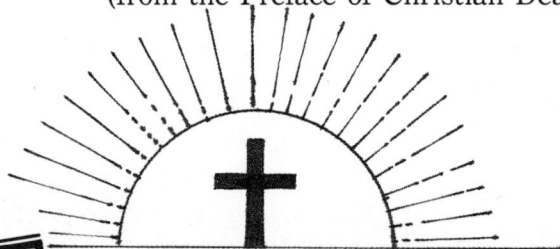

Extension work

A

Analyse the story. Can you give some of the reasons why Christians hold a funeral service? (Clue: examine what Father Tom says in his sermon.)

B

Research the Christian feast days called All Saints or All Hallows (1st November) and All Souls (2nd November). Which Christian beliefs about life after death are celebrated by these feasts?

ASSESS your work!

Tasks 14-21

1. *What view of suffering did you find in the Old Testament passage you studied?*
2. *What was Jesus' response to suffering and pain?*
3. *Why do Christians pray for those who are sick and near death?*
4. *What did you learn about the Sacrament of the Sick?*
5. *What did you learn about Jesus' suffering and death?*
6. *Why do Christians go on pilgrimage to places like Lourdes?*
7. *What is the significance of Lent for Christians?*
8. *Did you reflect on the meaning of Easter for Christians? Can you explain the meaning of the symbols used at the Easter Vigil?*
9. *In general how have you tackled the reflection exercises in this section?*

Review your work in the module

Pain, suffering, and death are not very happy areas to be thought about but they are too important to ignore. It seems unlikely that anyone could get through a normal life without some experience of pain or suffering, and death is an experience that comes to everybody in time.

- How did you feel doing this module?

- Do you find these aspects of life easy to reflect on or troublesome and difficult?

- Was the mood of your class any different during the time you were working on this module?

- This can be a difficult module to do, so if you have completed it, *very well done!*

Just before you finish off – review how you are managing your learning. . .

Managing your own learning

We are the Champions!

Were you
1. Usually on time for class/usually late for class?
2. Hardworking . . . most of the time/some of the time/not very often?
3. Able to work by yourself sometimes?
4. Able to work with others in a group?

Did you
5. Find the work very easy or very difficult?
6. Work when the teacher was busy with other people or only when the teacher was with you?
7. Cooperate with the teacher?
8. Did you follow up any of the work you did at home by reading or finding out more about any of the topics you have covered?
9. Did you do any extension/project work?

Do you
10. Find it easy to tell the teacher of any problems you had?
11. Prefer to work by yourself or with others?

Now, share what you have done with your class teacher.

Congratulations!

You have now completed *Celebration*, **Level Three.**

This module in your R.E. programme is called

Values *Level Three*

It is all about reflecting on the tensions that may exist between individuals and groups where there are different values, and about ways of dealing with differences.

The second half of the module will encourage you to reflect on how values are connected with what people believe and what they do in two of the major religious traditions, Islam and Christianity, particularly with reference to marriage and family life.

When you have finished working on this module, you should have:

- **reflected** on prejudice.

- **considered** some positive ways of dealing with differences.

- **reflected** on how Islamic and Christian values relate to beliefs, especially in relation to marriage and family life.

- **developed** self-confidence by having an informed and reflective attitude to questions of conflict and reconciliation.

Here are some of the activities you will be engaged in:

- **reflecting** on your own experience of changing values.

- **considering** some cases where values are in conflict.

- **examining the causes and effects** of prejudice.

- **reflecting** on strategies for dealing with prejudice.

- **reflecting** on the experience of young people in a Third-World setting.

- **considering** how Muslim and Christian values relate to belief and practice.

- **examining** Muslim and Christian values with regard to marriage and family life.

- **assessing your progress** in the learning involved in this module.

- **completing** the "managing your own learning" procedures and contributing to your profile for the work in this module.

Before you get weaving on this module, three points to look at:

1. This programme of religious education has four strands of experience which you will be weaving together:

   - The experience of home and family.
   - The experience of your local community.
   - The experience of community as **plural**, that is, involving a variety of different beliefs and traditions.
   - The experience of world-wide or **Global** community.

   We have used the following symbols to represent each of these strands:

2. If you have previously studied Level One and Level Two of Values, you may need to pick up some of the threads from those earlier modules.

   If this is the first Values' module you have worked on, you could use the rest of this page as a brief scene-setter for the module.

   Level One

   - What are "values"?
   - What is really important for you?
                         for your school?
                         for your local community?
   - What do TV, newspapers, advertising and the pop-world tend to value most?
   - What is really important for Hindus?
   - What is really important for Christians?

   Level Two

   - Give an example of a **moral** choice or decision.
   - What is meant by "responsibility"?
   - What is meant by "conscience"?
   - What are the main responsiblities of a member of the Jewish faith?
   - What do Christians mean by the word "stewardship"?

3. You may need to do some forward planning, with your teacher, for activities coming up later in this module.

   Look through and check if anything needs to be arranged.

   Your teacher will help you to organise this planning.

   You may also be adding some special activities to this module and leaving out those for which there is not time. Again, your teacher will help you with this.

> This R.E. programme is designed to help you to learn, so while it may involve hard work, it should also be fun to do. So, enjoy doing this module.

Changing values
reflecting on change

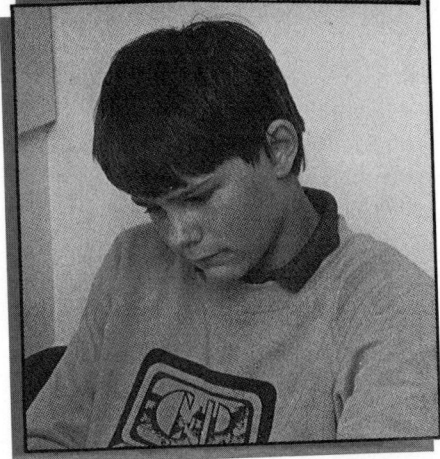

Task 1

IMAGINE: four snapshots in your family album:

you at 5 years old
you at 9 years old
you at 11 years old
you at 13–14 years old

Reflect

In what ways have you:

changed	stayed the same
_____	_____
_____	_____
_____	_____
_____	_____

Make a chart like this in your workbook or file, and fill it in.

Compare what you have written with what your partner has written.

Exchange your ideas about the way your partner has changed or stayed the same in the time you have known each other.

Reflect: what was most important for you (your values), at each of the stages in your life that you have been thinking and talking about?

Extension work

A

Analyse what has changed and what has remained the same about your values at each stage.

B

Analyse and _reflect_ on why some of your values changed – why are different things important for you now than before? How have these changes come about? Why are some things just as important now as before? Why have they not changed?

Values at home and in your family

Celia was not pleased.
Usually when Uncle Bill and Auntie Joyce came to visit, she went out the back door to her friends while they were ringing the front door bell. Today they had knocked at the kitchen door while the family were having tea. There was no escape!

"Celia, turn the TV off, dear, it's bad manners when you've got visitors," her mum had said.

Now they were sitting in the living room and Uncle Bill had finished telling his latest jokes. There was a lull, then Auntie Joyce spotted the family photo album on the table and started leafing through it.

"My word, haven't you grown, Celia! Look at you here – what a lovely little girl! Oh, that looks a nice place. Where was that taken, Edna?"

"We were camping in Scotland," Celia's mum said. "We used to go for weekends before George got his new job. Of course, George's parents were alive then, and we used to go and visit them. Once they died and George started working weekends and Celia joined the gymnastics club on Saturdays, that was the end of that."

"That reminds me" said Uncle Bill, "have you heard the one about . . .?"

Task 2

Reflect *on ways that your family has changed or stayed the same over the past years up till the present time. What was important for your family when you were very small; starting school; changing school?*

Compare *that with now.*

Talk *about this with your partner.*

Remember: *there might be things that have happened that you feel are very personal and private, and not to be talked about in school. That's fine. Perhaps there are some changes that you can talk about comfortably – that's up to you to decide.*

Extension work

A

Reflect: based on what you have each been thinking about, do you think that for most families, and speaking generally, there are some values that change and some that stay the same?

B

Reflect: do you think families today are similar or different to, say 30 or 40 years ago?

What evidence is there that attitudes have changed or stayed the same?

Do you think that families today consider the same or different things to be important compared with then?

Who could you ask, to find out about this?

A world of difference – or just the same?

Task 3

With your partner: thinking about the last fourteen years, identify what has changed, and what has remained the same, about the world you live in.

Make a chart like this one in your workbook or file, and fill it in.

Find an example which illustrates each of the following statements.

Some changes make things **better**.

Some changes make things **worse**.

Staying the same is sometimes a **good** thing.

Staying the same is sometimes a **bad** thing.

Now **reflect** *on your discussion of what has changed and what has remained the same, and* **highlight** *or* **underline** *or* **put a plus-sign** (+)

	CHANGED	SAME
Science		
Fashion		
Travel		
Transport		
Music		
TV and films		
Food		
Your town		
Sport		
Leisure		
Work		
Living standards		
Relationships		
Education		
Your country		
Religion		

on your chart next to those changes for the **better** *and aspects which are unchanged and remain, in your view,* **good**.

Extension work

A

Role-play a discussion between people who think that the world has changed completely where values are concerned and people who think that basically things are much the same as ever.
or
Write a song or poem entitled "Fings ain't wot they used to be" or "It's the same today as always".

B

Reflect: what factors (causes) have brought about the changes you have identified.

What factors have helped things to stay the same?

Moral qualities

Task 4 GROUP WORK

In your group, consider each of the following moral qualities and, having talked to your parents and adult friends and relatives, discuss whether you think young people today are, generally speaking, more or less:

honest   generous   trustworthy
truthful   caring   responsible

than young people, say, 20 years ago, when your parents were youngsters.

In your discussion, **note down** *how you think you are different from a youngster 20 years ago, if at all, and how you think you are the same, if at all.*

For homework: *find out if any of the adults at home agree with your conclusions!*

Extension work

A

Consider the two points-of-view in the cartoon and explain why the people in the cartoon might think that way.

> Nobody cares anymore:— It wasn't like this in my day

> If people of your generation had cared more, we wouldn't be in the mess we are in today!

B

Present evidence to support the conclusions arrived at in your group work on moral qualities.

Values in conflict

Case study

Imagine

Your school community is faced with a very difficult decision. A local high tech firm wants to buy the land next to your school to build a new factory. It will mean the school has no hockey, football, or athletics field, and there will be a certain amount of noise and danger from heavy vehicles making deliveries. The factory will cut off the view of the hills in the distance, and local community groups will lose the only sports field in the town.

However, the firm is offering enough money to allow the school to equip a new computer-based CDT suite, and promises to employ a number of school-leavers each year, as well as providing employment for many of the pupils' parents who are currently unemployed.

Task 5

In groups:

1. *Discuss the best way for the school to come to a decision about this offer.*

2. *Role-play a debate between those who support accepting the offer and those who recommend rejecting it in favour of keeping the sports facilities.*

Extension work

A

Find and *describe* any situation where there is a conflict of interests and of values that you know of in your community, or in the news. How would you resolve the problem?

B

Many of the parents, teachers, pupils and governors of the school in the story can see some value in both alternatives.

Describe the conflict of values that an individual in that situation might experience, and *reflect* on how he or she might reach a decision about it.

Dilemmas

Some conflicts are between groups who each have a clearly-defined goal or set of values in opposition to the others.

Dictionary work – look up **DILEMMA**

Sometimes, however, one person or group may experience a conflict of values, where there are two desirable choices but only one can be chosen, or where choosing to do something that you value damages or spoils something else which you value. This situation is called a dilemma – a split choice.

An example:

A parent from the school community in Task 5 has a daughter who is a very promising athlete and also extremely good at technical design. Which way should she vote? It's a dilemma!

To complicate things, the school in the next town has both a strong sports tradition and a good CDT block – but her daughter might not like to be separated from her friends and if she was lonely she might not do well. It's a dilemma!

Task 6

With your partner: make up some situations where there is a dilemma concerning the right thing to do.

Group work:

Pool your made-up dilemmas. Role-play each of them in turn.
Discuss possible ways of making the choice.

Extension work

A

Reflect on your own experience and the experience of people you know.

Have you or they ever had to make a choice where there were conflicting values?

How was the dilemma solved?

B

Reflect on some dilemmas involving human life or questions of right and wrong.

1. There is one kidney available for transplant but there is a young girl and the father of a family of three young children in need of it. What should the doctor do?

2. A mother discovers her son is a drug-dealer. Should she tell the police, knowing that her son will probably go to gaol?

3. Someone offers me a video recorder, very cheaply. I think it may be stolen but he says it isn't and I have no way of finding out. What should I do?

You may wish to contribute some examples of your own.

Changing values

a Third-World perspective

The Yanomani Indians live in the Calha Xlorte area of Brazil, surrounded by hundreds of miles of tropical rain forests, waterfalls and swollen rivers, an area twice the size of Switzerland. The land is rich in minerals – gold, diamonds, uranium and tin ore, and the forests are potentially valuable timber to be sold on world markets. The Yanomani hunt and fish there for survival. Over recent decades there has been a gold rush, with devastating effects on the land, and companies bull-dozing large areas of trees for timber. This industrial development has meant that roads were built and small towns grew up overnight. The people working for the firms brought with them measles, malaria and flu, which caused whole communities of the Yanomani to become ill and die. Davi Xiriana, one of their leaders, said "The presence of the road damaged our health, our traditions and our work". The estimated wealth of the minerals there is $120 bn. So there is no shortage of people who want to exploit this corner of Brazil. Now the army wants to build frontier posts all along the edge of this territory, to ensure defence from attack by other countries who might be tempted to occupy the land and steal its wealth. The churches and voluntary agencies in Brazil claim that what is happening will not just dispossess the Indians but will wipe them out as a people. "The only word to use is genocide," said an Italian missionary who has worked with the Yanomani for over 20 years.

For your information

The Yanomani live an outdoor life, hunting, fishing, cooking on a wood fire, eating meat, fish, bread, soup, fruit. They use river water to drink and as a place to swim and bathe. They paint their bodies with beautiful patterns using red dye and charcoal, and for special days wear feathers in their ears. In the evenings they lie in their hammocks and rest after the day's hunting and work. When somebody dies they cremate the body and then have a special feast to dispose of the ashes. They paint and decorate themselves and do the Dance of Presentation and spend several days drinking soup, eating, dancing and talking. It is also a time to trade and to argue, and the feast ends with bread and meat being given to all the guests before they go home.

Task 7

Role-play the scene at a meeting of the Yanomani with:

- Prospectors who wish to expand their mining sites.
- Generals who wish to build army posts, camps and possibly roads and services.
- Timber merchants who wish to continue felling trees over large areas.
- Church workers who wish to help the Yanomani to survive and preserve their traditions.

You need first to find out something of the lifestyle and traditions of the Yanomani.

Extension work

A GROUP WORK

If your group was the government of Brazil, what would you do in this situation?

B

Reflect: are there any other examples you can think of, of places where the values of a community are threatened by "progress"?

Tasks 1–7

1. *Did you work on your own, with your partner and with your group in doing Tasks 1–4?*

2. *What conclusions did you reach in Task 1 reflecting on change? Do you think you have changed a lot?*

3. *Did you enjoy thinking about how things change for families?*

4. *What did you learn from Task 3 about change in your local and wider world?*

5. *Do you think people care more, less, or just the same as in the past? Did your work on Task 4 help you to decide?*

6. *What did you learn from your study of dilemmas?*

7. *What have you learned from your study of the Yanomani Indians?*

8. *Are you enjoying this module so far? Say why or why not.*

9. *What could be improved – in this module? – in your response to this work?*

Recognising differences and finding common ground

So far in this module you have considered the idea of changing and conflicting values, or dilemmas. In the next section you are going to be looking at the values that people attach to similarities and differences.

Task 8 — Working on your own

Get a mental image (picture in your mind's eye) of your best friend or someone you know quite well. Now, make a chart in your work-book or file, like the one below:

	Me and my friend/acquaintance
Similarities	
Differences	

Identify *the ways in which you are similar.*
Identify *the ways in which you are different.*

When you have done this, analyse or categorize (group together) the similarities and differences.

For example:
light hair/dark hair, fair skin/sallow skin, blue eyes/brown eyes are all differences relating to **appearance** while:
mischievous, happy-go-lucky, lively
are similarities relating to **personality** or **character**.

*Now **reflect**: which similarities and differences, if any, are relatively unimportant in your view and which are important ones. Why?*

Extension work

A Reflect

Do you think you need to be basically similar to somebody before you can be good friends?

Do you think you can be good friends with somebody whom you think is basically different from you?

B Reflect

What would the world be like if people were all the same?

Write a short poem valuing difference.

or

Write a short story about a world where everybody is exactly the same.

Valuing different experiences

In the next section you will be looking at how communities deal with differences and similarities in people's experiences. Before you do, you need to examine some important words which are connected with this area of your work:

Prejudice: making up your mind about somebody on the basis of false or irrelevant evidence, or before finding out the necessary facts, e.g.

66 I don't like people from that part of town – I haven't met any but if I did I'm sure I wouldn't like them! **99**

Discrimination: to take action against somebody on the basis of a particular difference.

If the differences were **relevant** then the discrimination might be fair, e.g.

66 Only people with tickets will be admitted to the all-ticket Cup Final or Pop Concert – people who have not paid for tickets will not be allowed in. **99**

But if the differences are irrelevant it will result in unfair discrimination, e.g.

66 Only people with fair hair or blue eyes will be allowed into the concert. **99**

Extension work

A

Look for some examples of discrimination against people in your community on grounds of:

● Old age. ● Youth.

Research the work of Help the Aged, which cares for the elderly in many Third World countries as well as in Britain.

Task 9

Reflecting on attitudes to the elderly

Identify *the image which people in your group have of elderly people.*

Group work

Discuss and complete the following table in your group.

Elderly means ...
Elderly people are ...
The difficulties experienced by elderly people are ...
The main differences between elderly and young people are ...
What people enjoy about being elderly is ...
The contribution that elderly people make to society is ...

Identify *how some elderly people in your community feel about being elderly. What sort of attitudes do they encounter?*

What do they expect of the community? Many elderly people are grandparents – what do they have to offer families?

Reflect: *How accurate was the image your group explored at the beginning of this task?*

How safe is it to say
"The elderly **usually** . . . etc."
"The elderly are **generally** . . . etc."

B

Many people retire from work much earlier than used to be the case, and may live to a greater age than used to be the case.

Reflect: what difficulties and opportunities does this situation create? How should people approaching retirement prepare for this part of their lives?

Explore: the work of an organisation promoting an active life in retirement.

Reflect: the major religious traditions have all valued the role of elderly people as leaders of the community.

Why do you think this is so?

Reflecting on gender

Explore your attitudes and ideas about gender.

On your own, consider the following list of jobs, chores, activities and interests, and decide whether each one is better suited to boys/men or girls/women or equally suited to both.

	Girls/Women	Boys/Men	Both
Vacuuming			
Football			
Knitting			
Washing-up			
Ironing			
Car maintenance			
Nuclear physics			
Changing a baby's nappy			
Drinking a pint of beer			
Wearing jewellery			
Shopping			
Cooking			
Being a secretary			
Babysitting			
Proposing marriage			
Cricket			
Ballet dancing			
Decorating			
Plumbing			
Digging the garden			
Crying			
Being tough			

Group work

Compare *your answers in your groups, and see if your group can reach agreement.*

If you cannot agree, **examine the reasons** *why each of you thinks the way that you do.*

Is there any difference in the way that boys and girls feel about the list?

Extension work

A

Reflect: can you think of any situations where your group thinks that boys and girls should be treated differently?

Can you think of any situations where boys and girls are treated differently but you think that they should be treated on the same basis?

B

Following your discussion and reflection, do you think there are any attitudes that might need to be changed? If so, how would you go about doing that?

Prejudice and discrimination

You have looked at what these words mean already – in this section you are going to reflect on how people discriminate against different kinds of people, and the prejudices (unfair thoughts, feelings, and beliefs) that their actions are based on.

Extension work

A

Reflect: do you think you have ever been judged or discriminated against unfairly? *Describe* what happened. How did you feel? What did you think about the person who was responsible?

B

Reflect: imagine the situation of someone who is a victim of prejudice and discrimination of one of the kinds your have considered in your list. Pretend that you are that person and describe your thoughts and feelings.

Task 11

Reflect *on the causes of prejudice and discrimination.*

People might be prejudiced against others because

They think of the others as being different.

They are afraid of them.

They simply dislike or even hate the others.

They think of the others as being inferior.

They are ignorant about the others.

They identify with one group to the exclusion of others.

Can you think of any other causes of prejudice?

A person who has prejudice against someone else may put their prejudice into action – by discriminating unfairly against that person.

There are lots of different types of prejudice – see if you can think of an example for each type in the chart below.

	Prejudice (beliefs)	Discrimination (action)
Age		
Gender		
Lifestyle		
Race		
Religion		
Class or status		
Disability	e.g. "disabled people are not normal."	Not to allow disabled people to attend schools or be employed like others.
Nationality		

63

Dealing with differences

Role-play

With you partner imagine a situation where two people have a serious disagreement over something. How are they going to deal with their differences? What strategies (approaches) could they use to resolve things?

Role-play some different approaches.

Confrontation – a head-on clash involving rows and possibly even violence. Neither party wants to give in, and tries to force the other into agreeing.

Coexistence – avoiding confrontation but ignoring the differences and pretending that the other doesn't exist.

'Let sleeping dogs lie.'

Dialogue – an attempt to build bridges with the other person, being prepared both to talk and to listen, to spend time together, to recognise that the other person has a point of view, to learn from the other person, to try to reach agreement in the light of shared experience and to make allowances for, and to learn from, differences.

Now **read** *this story.*

Extension work

A

Analyse: which of these strategies did Carla's family use?

Which was the most effective in the end?

Reflect: have you ever been in a situation like this?

How did you tackle your differences?

Do you prefer confrontation, coexistence or dialogue?

B

Analyse: are there any situations in your school or district where some of these strategies are being used?

Or have you heard of something in the news which involves one of these ways of dealing with serious differences?

Reflect: thinking globally, which approach seems most likely to make for progress, do you think?

Carla knew there was going to be trouble. She was supposed to be back from the Youth Club at nine o'clock, but she had chatted to her friends a bit too long, missed the bus and had to walk home. Dad would be furious. As she pressed the doorbell, she knew what was coming.

"That's the last time you're going to that club of an evening young lady, and make no mistake about it!"

"You can't stop me going just because I was late once."

"Oh can't I – well, we'll see, and less of your cheek. I don't like your attitude these days – you never think that me and your mum will be worried. It's one time too many and you're not going again – that's final."

Mum said nothing. In fact, she said nothing for a few days. She didn't want a row with Carla but she thought dad was right really. In the end, Carla couldn't stand the tension any longer. She waited for the right moment one evening to try a different tack.

"Look, dad, I know you were worried about me the other night and I'm sorry for getting you and mum upset. It was my fault I missed the bus but I didn't do it on purpose and it won't happen again. I love going to the club and meeting my friends and there's nothing much else to do around here, is there?"

"You'd better get a move on then," said dad, "that bus goes in three minutes – but think on!"

Learning from diversity

In the last few tasks you have been looking at how differences between people may lead to difficulties where there is fear or aggression or lack of understanding. In this task, you will be reflecting on the possibility of learning from differences and being enriched by meeting people with a variety of different beliefs, customs and lifestyles.

"Weaving the Web" is an R.E. programme in which you are encouraged to weave some different strands of experience into how you see life.

Extension work

A

Compare what you are doing in R.E. with what your parents or the people at home did when they were at school. What do they say about it?

B

Consider whether understanding the differences between groups pushes them further apart or brings them closer together.

Task 13 — Reflecting on differences

Group work

This task is an opportunity to think about the work you have been doing in your R.E. programme. In your group, think about the different experiences of community that you have been exploring:

Different experiences of family and home life.

Different experiences of living in your local community.

Different customs and traditions that you have explored.

The experience of living in different communities in different parts of the world.

1. *Do you think it is a good idea to study a variety of people, beliefs and lifestyles?*
2. *What does your group think it has learned from this exploration?*
3. *What difference would it make if you **only** studied the communities you already had the most contact with or experience of, e.g. your own family, school and street, or religious group?*
4. *What benefits do you think you might get from your study in later life?*
5. *Does your group think that any of its attitudes have changed from looking at different beliefs and lifestyles?*
6. *How do you think your own beliefs, understanding and feelings might have been deepened or enriched by what you have learnt?*
7. *Has all this helped you to understand more about your own beliefs and lifestyle?*

Tasks 8 – 13

1. *What do you think is good about the fact that there are lots of differences between people?*

2. *What have you learnt about the possible difficulties that differences may give rise to?*

3. *What did you learn in your reflection on the elderly in your community?*

4. *What sort of attitudes did you find in your work on gender?*

5. *Do you know now what prejudice and discrimination are?*

6. *How do you generally deal with situations where you have a markedly different view from some others?*

7. *What was the general conclusion of your evaluation in Task 13?*

Values in Islam – beliefs

So far in this module, you have been reflecting on how what people do, the values they live by, are based on what they believe. In this task, you will be exploring the beliefs which Muslims have which give rise to the values they live by.

Task 14

Learning about beliefs in Islam

Can you match up the following statements with the basic beliefs of Islam. Which is tauhid, khilafah, or akhrah?

Allah is our judge . . .

The world is green and beautiful . . .

. . . God has appointed you his stewards over it.

There is one God, Allah, and Muhammad is His Prophet.

Whoever plants a tree and diligently looks after it until it matures and bears fruit . . .

. . . is rewarded.

Razwana's story

" My name is Razwana. I'm 13 and I live in Leeds in Yorkshire. I am a Muslim and after being at school during the daytime, I go some days to the Qur'ānic classes at the mosque. Last week at my comprehensive school, my teacher asked me if I would like to tell people in my class about the basic beliefs of Islam. That evening I checked with my religious teacher at the mosque that I had got things right, then I had this brill idea – I asked Miss if I could do a sort of worksheet and she said, even better, she'd put it on an overhead projector sheet. Next day I stood next to the projector with my diagram projected on the wall behind me, and I felt nervous but a bit like Miss when she teaches us. Here's the overhead. **"**

Tauhid
The Unity of god and Creation

Khilafah
The world is entrusted to us as stewards

Akhrah
We will be judged on how we cared for what God has given

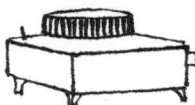

Extension work

A

If, like Muslims, you believed in **tauhid**, **khilafah** and **akhrah**, how do you think you should live and act? List a few basic rules that would help you live out your beliefs.

B

If you were asked to state some basic beliefs which would help people live well and make the world a better place, what would you say? *List* and *describe* some of these basic beliefs.

Compare them with what others in the class have written.

Values in Islam – action

Muslims believe that faith in God without action is of no use; Muslims must both believe in God and act accordingly. The values by which a Muslim lives must be seen in action every day. The religion of Islam is compared to a building built on five pillars, each of which is a duty and a value for followers of Islam.

| FAITH | FASTING | PRAYER | GIVING TO THE POOR | PILGRIMAGE |
| (Shahadah) | (Saum) | (Salat) | (Zakat) | (Hajj) |

You have explored the main elements of Islamic belief in the last task, summed up in the **kalimah**:

66 There is no God but Allah and Muhammad is Allah's Messenger. **99**

In other modules at Level Three you have explored fasting, pilgrimage and prayer in Islam. In this task, you will be reflecting on the duty of Muslims to give to the poor, a duty called **zakat**.

Razwana's father, Abdullah, explains:

66 When my son Khaliq was given his name at the naming ceremony in the mosque, his baby hair was shaved off his head and weighed, and we had to give an equivalent amount of money to charity. Muslims believe that they have a duty to share some of their wealth with those who are poorer than themselves. In the mosque there is a box marked **zakat** where people who are worshipping can put an offering to help the poor, not just at special times but regularly. You see, we believe that the goods of this world are given to us by God and we are entrusted with

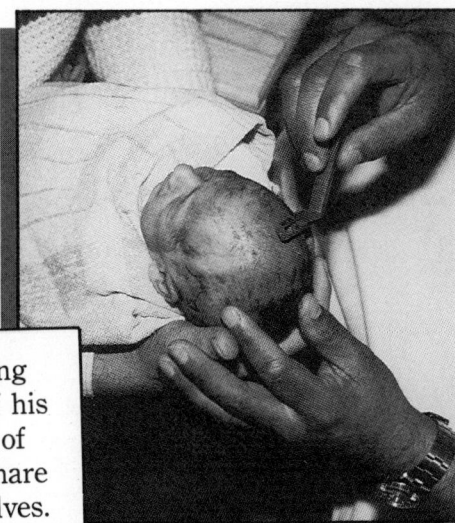

them to put them to good use. By sharing in this way, we show our commitment to our brothers and sisters in the community; that our community is like one family, God's people. Muhammad said 'He who eats his fill while his brother is hungry cannot be a Muslim.' We would be judged as sinners if we ignored the poor and needy. We have a guide for how much we should give. We work out what we need for our income for daily life, and then we give a percentage of what is left to the poor. **"**

Extension work

A

Find out what Muslims and/or members of other traditions are doing to help people in need in your community.

B

Do you think those who are poor or in need should be looked after by the State only, or by charity only, or by both together? Say why.

Task 15

Analyse: *can you recognise the three central beliefs of Islam (task) in Abdullah's account of Zakat?*

Reflect: *do you think there are any reasons why people who are not Muslims should give a share of their wealth to poorer people?*

What reasons might people who do not believe in God give for helping others in need?

Values in Islam – *marriage and family life*

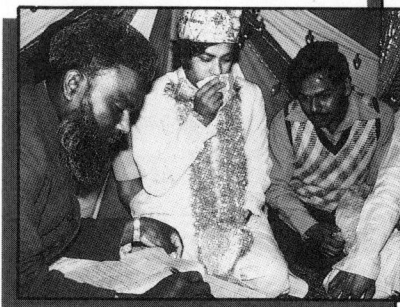

Quasim and Surriya's Wedding

Razwana's cousin, Quasim, married Surriya only a short time ago. They had known each other quite a long time but their engagement was arranged through their parents. Quasim told his mother that he was attracted to Surriya and his mother had many meetings with Surriya's family to see if they were suited to each other. Muslims believe that married people know best about marriage and the qualities it demands. When their parents decided it would be a good marriage, Quasim and Surriya were very pleased — Surriya could have said no to the wedding, but she was happy to agree to be married. Quasim's family collected together the money and presents which would be given to Surriya as a dowry — a way of giving practical help and security to the bride and her family. The dowry, or **mahr**, becomes the property of the bride, showing that Quasim recognises Surriya as a person worthy of respect.

The wedding took place, not in a mosque, but in Surriya's home. At Quasim's house, guests were welcomed and prayers said, and Quasim's head was covered with a very intricate head-dress, and the guests pinned money to his clothes. Then the whole family and guests set off with Quasim to Surriya's house for the wedding.

Quasim and Surriya stayed in separate rooms during the ceremony. Quasim made his marriage vows and the witnesses went to tell Surriya that this had been done. Then Surriya made her vows and Quasim was informed. The marriage certificate was signed in each of the rooms. Then a wedding ring was placed on Quasim's finger. At this point, young women, friends of Surriya, brought a plate of traditional sweetmeats and a glass of milk for Quasim — a sign that those present hoped that the marriage would produce children. Quasim and Surriya were now married and with the families and guests went off to celebrate at a reception in a community hall nearby.

Extension work

A

Reflect: what help do you think young people need, if any, in choosing a marriage partner and getting married?

B

Compare and *contrast* this account with a wedding you have attended.

Values in Christianity – beliefs

Did you complete Story Level Two? If you did, do you remember The Ten Commandments – basic rules for a good life?

If your work in the Story Level Two is available, have a look at what you actually did.

Jesus accepted the commandments of the Old Testament. He also summed them up in the Two Laws of Love. Do you remember them from Story Level Two? Look back to remind yourself. (Story Level Two p. 42 and p. 47)

Now continue your work on this module.

James and Margaret took their baby along to their local parish church to be baptised. Their families and friends went with them. This was to be the day when their young child became a member of the church community. (You can read all about what happens at a baptism in Level One, Community, p. 22.) After the first prayers and readings, and before baptising the baby, the priest asked James and Margaret if they fully understood what they were asking for their baby. They both said they wanted young Sarah to become a member of the Christian community through baptism. Of course, Sarah was not old enough yet to make the prayers or promises for herself, so her parents were speaking on her behalf, asking that she be brought up in the faith which her family and parents shared. The priest then asked James and Margaret and their guests to declare openly what they believed, by answering the baptismal creed (the beliefs and promises of being a Christian). Here is what was said:

Extract from Roman Catholic baptism

Celebrant

Dear parents and godparents:
You have come here to present this child for baptism. By water and the Holy Spirit she is to receive the gift of new life from God, who is love.

If your faith makes you ready to accept this responsibility, renew now the vows of your own baptism. Reject sin; profess your faith in Christ Jesus. This is the faith of the Church. This is the faith in which this child is about to be baptized.

Celebrant

Do you reject sin, so as to live in the freedom of God's children?

Parents and **Godparents** I do

Celebrant

Do you reject the glamour of evil, and refuse to be mastered by sin?

Parents and **Godparents** I do

69

In the Roman Catholic tradition the same beliefs are declared at Easter time and during confirmation.

Task 17

Read the baptismal promises and **analyse** *them – make a summary of the basic beliefs and put them in your own words.*

Reflect: *on what you have done and try to explain to your partner what Christians basically believe.*

Extension work

A

Make a chart or visual display of the central beliefs of Christians. Here are some words to help you – you may think of others:

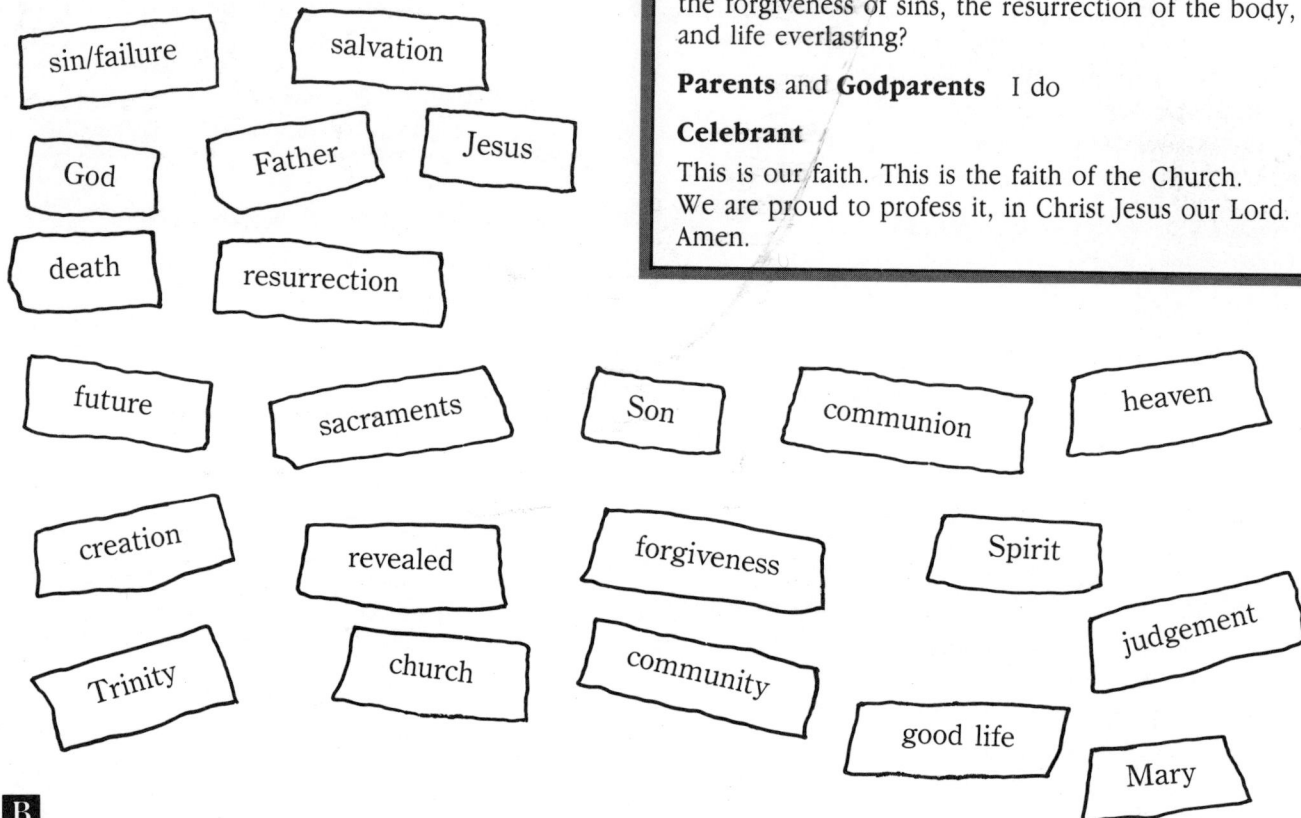

sin/failure

salvation

God

Father

Jesus

death

resurrection

future

sacraments

Son

communion

heaven

creation

revealed

forgiveness

Spirit

Trinity

church

community

good life

judgement

Mary

Celebrant

Do you reject Satan, father of sin and prince of darkness?

Parents and **Godparents**   I do

Celebrant

Do you believe in God, the Father almighty, creator of heaven and earth?

Parents and **Godparents**   I do

Celebrant

Do you believe in Jesus Christ, his only Son, our Lord,
who was born of the Virgin Mary,
was crucified, died, and was buried,
rose from the dead,
and is now seated at the right hand of the Father?

Parents and **Godparents**   I do

Celebrant

Do you believe in the Holy Spirit,
the holy Catholic Church, the communion of saints,
the forgiveness of sins, the resurrection of the body,
and life everlasting?

Parents and **Godparents**   I do

Celebrant

This is our faith. This is the faith of the Church.
We are proud to profess it, in Christ Jesus our Lord.
Amen.

B

Interview an adult Christian and ask about their beliefs. *Compare* this with the baptismal promises in Task 16 or with the Creed used in a Eucharist.

or

Examine some slides or pictures of images of Jesus in Christian art.

What do they tell you about what Christians believe?

Values in Christianity – a case study

> " My name is Gerard. I work in a garage as a fitter in the East End of London. I play for a team in the local football league on Saturdays and I enjoy going out at weekends with my friends. Being a Christian means a lot to me. It's not just about having certain beliefs, although believing is important, and without faith, the rest doesn't make much sense. It's a way of life. Personally, I look to Jesus as a guide for how to live my life, and help when things get difficult. More than that – Jesus is with me in a real way, helping me to overcome my failings and come close to God. I spend a little time each week reading the gospels, and I always make time for some peace and quiet and to be by myself. That helps me to get on better with other people and to help out where I can. On Sunday, I worship at my local parish church. I feel a part of the community there and I join in a lot of the social events and the work for charity. Through the readings and sermons, I carry on learning more about my faith and how it works in practice. It's a support to be part of a community which shares your beliefs and guides you with its teachings – but of course you still have to be responsible for what you do and how you treat other people. Being a Christian has made me much more aware of people who struggle to get what they need to live on, or to have the same chance as me of a happy life. "

Task 18

Explore *what being a Christian means to Gerard; what are his values?*

Analyse: *why does Gerard have these values? Where do they come from? Where does he get support and encouragement for his way of life?*

Reflect: *what difference does being a Christian make to Gerard's life?*

Extension work

A

If you know any Christians, *compare* Gerard's values, lifestyle and beliefs with theirs. What similarities and differences are there?

B

Gerard is, in fact, a member of a Pentecostal church. You might like to try and *find out* something more about that particular form of Christianity.

Reflect: if Gerard had been, say, a Roman Catholic, what do you think would have been the same, what different, in his account of his faith and lifestyle?

Christian values – commitment to life as a single person

In the task after this you will be exploring how Christians view marriage and family life. Before you do that, you are invited to explore how people who choose to remain single view their way of life in the light of their religious faith.

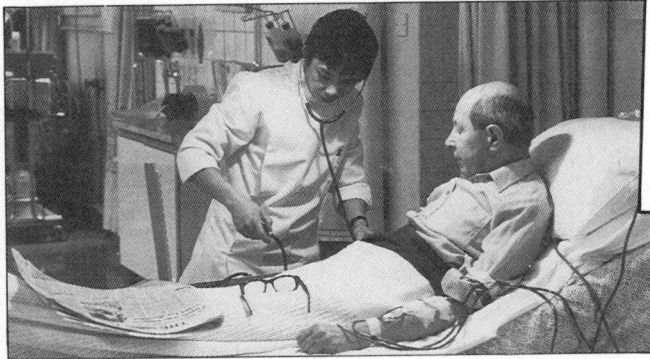

Helen – teacher

"I suppose I've always wanted to be a teacher. I gave myself to it full-time, and I'm sure I'm able to get involved more than if I had to go home to be with my own family. In a way, without being soppy, the kids here are my family and I'm sure that I'm using my talents in the way that God would want me to."

Colin – male nurse

"I live a very full life, and I work long hours in the hospital. I enjoy the quiet of my flat and a lively social life, which helps me to keep going when it gets difficult, especially in Casualty and on the cancer ward. Being single makes it easy for me to go and stay at my mum's if she's not too well or at Christmas time when she's missing dad all the more."

Anita – works for Voluntary Service Overseas

"I may get married some day – I'm sure I'd make a good parent – but I'm very involved in the work here in Sudan, and I'm very happy to be doing this at the moment. Who knows, I may still be here or somewhere similar many years from now."

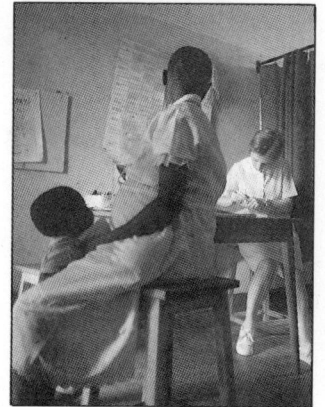

Task 19 Group work

Reflect: *what do you think people who remain single may offer to the life of the community?*

What do you think are attractive aspects of remaining single?

What do you think would be challenging or difficult aspects of being single?

Dictionary work
Vocation – a sense of being called by God to live a certain kind of life.

Extension work

A

Ask a member of a religious order living a celibate but community life to speak to your class about his/her vocation and way of life.

Plan what you will ask and how you will record what you learn.

B

Make a study of a person who has commited his/her life to service of the wider community while remaining single. *Compare* his/her achievements, commitment and struggles, with your reflections in Task 19.

Christian marriage

When Stephen and Lisa, who are Catholics, decided to get married, they contacted their parish priest well in advance of their wedding day. This was so that they could attend the meetings arranged in their area for couples preparing for marriage. As one of the most important decisions and commitments they would undertake in life, their marriage had to be planned and prepared for carefully. At home they were planning for the wedding day, but at the meetings they were discussing with other young couples and with some long-married people issues concerned with committing themselves to each other for life, and how to deal with the difficulties they might meet in setting up home together.

> How would life be different for them?
> How would they manage their finances?
> Would they keep up their other interests?
> What differences would having children make?

Father Thomas helped them to prepare the marriage ceremony. He explained that for Catholics marriage is a sacrament, a way of sharing in God's love. Stephen and Lisa would be conferring marriage on each other, in the sight of God and with the church community, their families and friends, as witnesses and supporters. They would be a sign of God's love, to each other and to their friends and families.

Stephen and Lisa chose the readings from the Bible and the music and hymns for the service. On the day of their wedding, Stephen waited near the altar at the front of the church, while Lisa was escorted up the aisle by her father. She was followed by bridesmaids and Stephen's best friend, Joe, was Best Man.

The ceremony is a simple one. After being welcomed, listening to readings from the Bible, and being prayed for, Stephen and Lisa exchanged their marriage vows, confirming that there was no legal bar to their marriage, and promising themselves to each other for life. The vows mention both the happiness and the difficulties of this commitment:

> "For better, for worse,
> for richer, for poorer,
> in sickness and in health,
> to love and to cherish,
> till death do us part."

The couple then exchanged rings – the exchange was a symbol of giving themselves to each other, and the rings symbolised a promise of unending commitment and love for each other.

The ceremony also stresses that one of the purposes of marriage is to bring children into the world. The community prays for God's blessing on the couple both for their marriage and for their possible future as parents and teachers of their children.

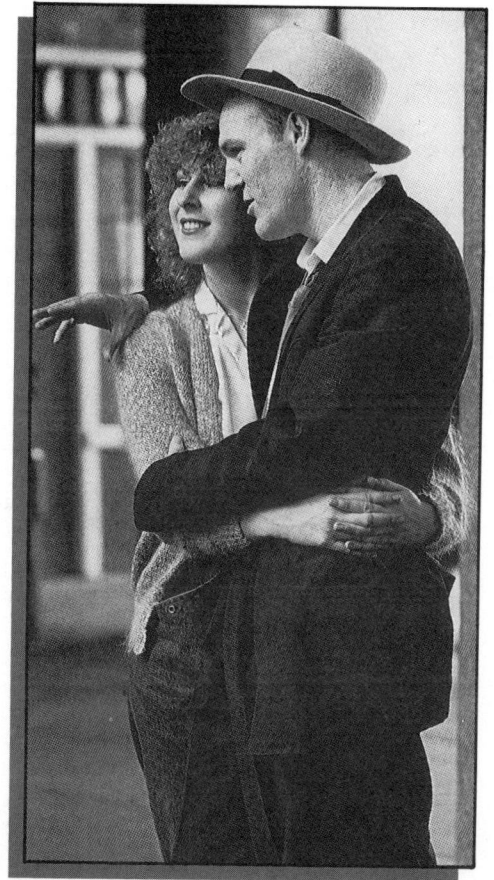

After saying the prayer, the "Our Father", Stephen and Lisa received a final blessing from Father Thomas, and went to sign the marriage register, which shows that the marriage is a legal contract recognised by the State.

Then they emerged to be congratulated by their families and friends, and to enjoy a party or "reception" in their honour. For Stephen and Lisa, it was the first day of their married life.

Final Blessing

Priest:
God the eternal Father keep you in love for each
    other,
so that the peace of Christ may stay with you
and be always in your home.
Amen.

May your children bless you,
your friends console you
and all men live in peace with you.
Amen.

May you always bear witness to the love of God
    in this world
so that the afflicted and the needy
will find in you generous friends,
and welcome you into the joys of heaven.
Amen.

From the Nuptial Blessing

Father, keep them always true to your
    commandments.
Keep them faithful in marriage.
and let them be living examples of Christian life.
Give them the strength which comes from the
    gospel
so that they may be witnesses of Christ to others.
        Bless them with children
        and help them to be good parents.

Task 20

Read the account of Stephen and Lisa's marriage, and identify the **values** *which the ceremony is based on.*

What qualities do you think people might need in order to be good husbands and wives, and good parents?

Extension work

A

Reflect: What do you think are the main difficulties which married people face?

How do they face up to these difficulties? What causes some marriages to break up?

B

Invite a marriage counsellor to speak to your class about the work he or she is involved in. Plan what you ask and how you will record what is said.

Tasks 14—20

1. *What beliefs would a person have to hold in order to be able to be called a Christian?*

2. *What are the three central beliefs of Islam?*

3. *From what you have learnt do you think a Christian would look upon their faith as largely a matter of going to Church?*

4. *What did you learn about the values Christians have?*

5. *From what you have learned, do you think there is any difference between marriage in a registry office and marriage in a Christian church? Explain your answer.*

6. *Did you reflect on people who stay single and how they might see their life as a special calling? What do you think?*

Review of the module

1. What are the values which this module considered?

2. Did you find you were reflecting on different kinds of attitudes? Which ones? Did any of your attitudes or ideas change while you were studying this module?

3. How did your groups take to the group work? Were they positive and constructive? Did they get the work done?

4. How would you sum up in a couple of sentences what you have learned from this module?

5. Was there anything you particularly enjoyed in it?

6. Did you think there was an approach, an experience or a visit that would have helped your learning?

Just before you finish off, how have you been doing in the course of your work?

Managing your own learning

We are the Champions!

Were you

1. Usually on time for class/usually late for class?
2. Hardworking ... most of the time/some of the time/not very often?
3. Able to work by yourself sometimes?
4. Able to work with others in a group?

Did you

5. Find the work very easy or very difficult?
6. Work when the teacher was busy with other people or only when the teacher was with you?
7. Cooperate with the teacher?
8. Did you follow up any of the work you did at home by reading or finding out more about any of the topics you have covered?
9. Did you do any extension/project work?

Do you

10. Find it easy to tell the teacher of any problems you had?
11. Prefer to work by yourself or with others?

Now, share what you have done with your class teacher.

Congratulations! **You have completed *Values*, Level Three.**

RELIGION IN LIFE

A Religious Education Course
for Secondary Schools

2. Founders, Prophets and Sacred Books

SCHOFIELD & SIMS LTD., HUDDERSFIELD

0 7217 3034 5
0 7217 3039 6 Net Edition

First printed 1985

Typesetting by PFB Art & Type Ltd., Leeds
Printed in England by Chorley & Pickersgill Ltd., Leeds